Jenny G
C000150080

Carrying on in Key Stage 1
# Sculpting,
## Stuffing and Squeezing

Published 2011 by A&C Black Publishers Limited
36 Soho Square, London W1D 3QY

**www.acblack.com**

ISBN 978-1-4081-3975-2

First published 2008 by Featherstone Education Ltd

Text © Ros Bayley, Lyn Broadbent, Sally Featherstone 2008

Photographs © Fotolia 2011, Shutterstock 2011

Additional photos © Lynn Broadbent, Ros Bayley, Sally Featherstone, Sarah Featherstone 2008, ASCO

Designed by Lynda Murray

A CIP record for this publication is available from the British Library.

All rights reserved. No part of this publication may be reproduced in any form or by any means - graphic, electronic, or mechanical, including photocopying, recording, taping or information storage or retrieval systems - without the prior permission in writing of the publishers.

Printed in Malta by Gutenburg Press Ltd

This book is produced using paper that is made from wood grown in managed, sustainable forests. It is natural, renewable and recyclable.

The logging and manufacturing processes conform to the environmental regulations of the country of origin.

To see our full range of titles visit **www.acblack.com**

# Contents

# Introduction

This series of books is intended to support the continuing growth and development of independent learning and practical activities, which are key features of the Early Years Foundation Stage (EYFS).

Children in Key Stage 1 need and deserve the chance to build on the best of practice in the EYFS, which carefully balances adult directed tasks with learning that children initiate and develop themselves, often in the company of responsive adults. These activities, which include sand and water play, construction, role play, independent mark making and writing, creative work, dance and movement, and outdoor play, are some of the activities children value most and miss most in Years 1 and 2.

This quote from a Year 1 boy echoes the feelings of many children who need a continuation of the learning styles and situations offered in Reception classes. However, many teachers in Key Stage One feel intense pressure to concentrate on activities that require recording and increasing levels of direction from adults. Why is this, and is it right for teachers to feel so pressured?

One thing we know from research is that practical activity and independent learning are essential for brain growth and reinforcement of growing abilities throughout childhood, at least until the onset of puberty, and for many children this is a lifelong need. We also know that the embedding of learning and the transformation of this into real understanding takes time and practice. Skills need to be reinforced by revisiting them in many different contexts in child-initiated learning and practical

challenges. Practical tasks in real life situations will be far more effective than rote learning, worksheets or adult direction.

It is also clear from brain research that many boys (and some girls) are just not ready by the end of Reception to embark on a formal curriculum which involves a lot of sitting down, listening and writing. Their bodies and their brains still need action, challenge and freedom to explore materials and resources.

But this does not mean that challenge should be absent from such activity! The brain feeds on challenge and novelty, so teachers and other adults working in Key Stage One need to structure the experiences, so they build on existing skills and previous activities, while presenting opportunities to explore familiar materials in new and exciting ways. Such challenges and activities can:

- be led by the Programme of Study for Key Stage 1
- focus on thinking skills and personal capabilities
- relate to real world situations and stimuli
- help children to achieve the five outcomes for Every Child Matters.

> 'I hear and I forget,
> I see and I remember,
> I do and I understand.'
>
> *Ancient Chinese Proverb*

## Every Child Matters

The five outcomes:

- ☐ Enjoy and achieve
- ☐ Stay safe
- ☐ Be healthy
- ☐ Make a positive contribution
- ☐ Achieve economic well-being

In **Carrying on in Key Stage 1**, we aim to give you the rationale, the process and the confidence to continue a practical, child-centred curriculum which also helps you as teachers to meet the requirements of the statutory curriculum for Key Stage One. Each book in the series follows the same format, and addresses objectives from many areas of the National Curriculum. Of course, when children work on practical challenges, curriculum elements become intertwined, and many will be going on simultaneously.

## The role of the adult

Of course, even during child-initiated learning, the role of the adult is crucial. Sensitive adults play many roles as they support, challenge and engage the children in their care. High quality teaching is not easy! If teachers want to expand experiences and enhance learning, they need to be able to stand back, to work alongside, and to extend or scaffold the children's learning by offering provocations and challenges to their thinking. The diagram on the right attempts to describe this complex task, and the way that adults move around the elements in the circle of learning. For ease of reading we have described the elements in the following way, and each double page spread covers all three of the vital roles adults play.

### Previous experience: recognising and building on the practical activities which children have experienced before

This element of the process is vital in scaffolding children's learning so it makes sense to them. Your knowledge of the Foundation Stage curriculum and the way it is organised will be vital in knowing where to start.

Teachers and other adults should have first hand knowledge of both the resources and the activities which have been available and how they have been offered in both child-initiated and adult-led activities. This knowledge should be gained by visiting the Reception classes in action, and by talking to adults and children as they work. Looking at Reception planning will also help.

### The responsive adult: Understanding the range of adult roles, and the effect different roles have on children's learning

Responsive adults react in different ways to what they see and hear during the day. This knowledge will influence the way they plan for further experiences to meet emerging needs and build on individual interests. The diagram illustrates the complex and interlinking ways in which adults interact with children's learning. Observing, co-playing and extending learning often happen simultaneously, flexibly and sometimes unconsciously. It is only when we reflect on our work with children that we realise what a complex and skilled activity is going on.

### Offering challenges and provocations

As the adults collect information about the learning, they begin to see how they can help children to extend and scaffold their thinking and learning. The adults offer challenges or provocations which act like grit in an oyster, provoking the children to produce responses and think in new ways about what they know and can do.

### Linking the learning with the skills and content of the curriculum

As the children grapple with new concepts and skills, adults can make direct links with curriculum intentions and content. These links can be mapped out across the range of knowledge, skills and understanding contained in the curriculum guidance for Key Stage One. It is also possible to map the development of thinking skills, personal capabilities and concepts which link the taught curriculum with the real world.

**The adult as extender of learning**
- discusses ideas
- shares thinking
- makes new possibilities evident
- instigates new opportunities for learning
- extends and builds on learning and interests
- supports children in making links in learning
- models new skills and techniques

**The adult as co-player**
- shares responsibility with the child
- offers suggestions
- asks open questions
- responds sensitively
- models and imitates
- plays alongside

**The adult as observer**
- listens attentively
- observes carefully
- records professionally
- interprets skilfully

As children plan, explore, invent, extend, construct, discuss, question and predict in the rich experiences planned and offered, they will communicate what they are learning through speech and actions, as well as through the outcomes of activities.

## Looking for the learning

Assessment for learning involves adults and children in sharing and analysing what they discover. Reflecting on learning, through discussion with other children and adults, is a key factor in securing skills and abilities, fixing and 'hard wiring' the learning in each child's brain. And, of course, teachers and other adults need to recognise, confirm and record children's achievements, both for the self esteem this brings to the children and to fulfil their own duties as educators.

You could find out what children already know and have experienced by:

- talking to them as individuals and in small groups

- talking to parents and other adults who know them well (teaching assistants are often wonderful sources of information about individual children)

- visiting the Reception classes and looking at spaces, storage and access to resources, including the use of these out of doors

- providing free access to materials and equipment and watching how children use them when you are not giving any guidance

- talking as a group or class about what children already know about the materials and those they particularly enjoy using.

**Using the curriculum grid to observe, to recognise learning and celebrate achievement**

At the end of this section you will find a photocopiable curriculum grid covering the whole Programme of Study for Key Stage 1 which can be used for planning and particularly for recording observations. This is a 'shorthand version' of the full grid included at the end of the book on pages 40-48.

We suggest that as the children work on the provocations and other challenges in this book, adults (teachers and teaching assistants) can use the grid to observe groups of children and record the areas of the curriculum they are covering in their work. The grid can also be used to record what children say and describe in plenary sessions and other discussions.

These observations will enable you to recognise the learning that happens as children explore the materials and engage with the challenging questions you ask and the problems you pose. And of course, as you observe, you will begin to see what needs to happen next; identifying the next steps in learning! This logical and vital stage in the process may identify:

- some children who will be ready for more of the same activity

- some who need to repeat and reinforce previous stages

- some who need to relate skills to new contexts, the same activity or skill practised in a new place or situation

- some who will want to extend or sustain the current activity in time, space or detail

- others who will wish to record their work in photos, drawings, models, stories, video and so on.

The grid also identifies the key skills which children need for thinking about and evaluating their work. Many schools now observe and evaluate how well these skills are developing when children work on challenging projects and investigations.

## Ready for more?

Offering extension activities is a way of scaffolding children's learning, taking the known into the unknown, the familiar into the new, the secure into the challenging. It is the role of the adult to turn their knowledge of the children into worthwhile, long-term lines of enquiry and development which will become self-sustaining and last throughout life.

At the end of each section in the book you will find a selection of useful resources, links and other information to help you support children in making structures, sculptures and other 3D creations. You could use these resources by encouraging individuals and groups:

- to use the Internet to find images and information

- to use ICT equipment such as cameras, tape recorders, video and dictaphones to record their explorations and experiments

- to explore information books in libraries and other places at home and at school

- to make contact by email and letter with experts, craftsmen, artists, manufacturers, suppliers and other contacts

- to make books, films, PowerPoint presentations

- to record their work in photographs and other media

- to respond to stimuli such as photographs, video, exhibitions and other creative stimuli

- to look at the built and natural environment with curiosity, interest and creativity

- to become involved in preserving the natural world, develop environmental awareness and support recycling

- to look at the world of work and extend their ideas of what they might become and how they might live their lives

- to develop a sense of economic awareness and the world of work in its widest sense

- to feel a sense of community and to explore how they might make a contribution to the school and wider communities in which they live

- to work together and develop the ability to think, reason and solve problems in their learning.

The suggested resources include websites, books, contacts and addresses. There are also some photographs which may inspire young learners as they work on the provocations and challenges suggested.

We hope you will find the ideas in this book useful in stimulating your work with children in Year 1 and Year 2. Before trying the activities please check for allergies and be aware of safety at all times. The ideas, photos and provocations we have included are only a start to your thinking and exploring together. Of course you and the children will have many more as you start to expand the work they do in these practical areas, providing a rich curriculum base using familiar and well loved materiaals.

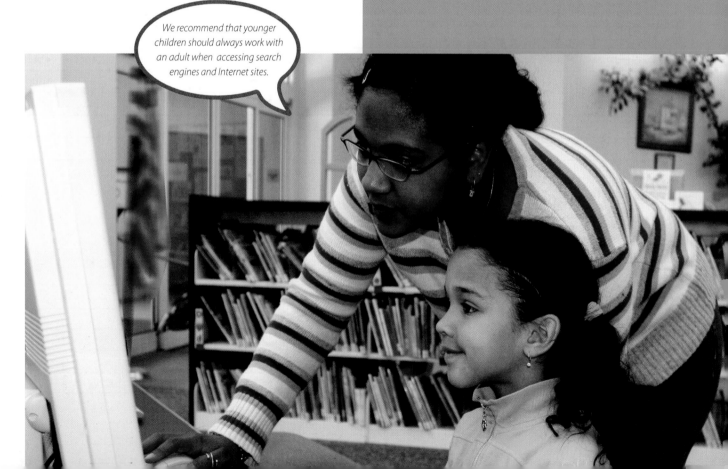

*We recommend that younger children should always work with an adult when accessing search engines and Internet sites.*

# Planning and observation of _____ (the activity)  Name: _____ Date: _____

## Literacy

| Lit 1 Speak | Lit 2 Listen | Lit 3 Group | Lit 4 Drama | Lit 5 Word | Lit 6 Spell | Lit 7 Text 1 | Lit 8 Text 2 | Lit 9 Text 3 | Lit 10 Text 4 | Lit 11 Sentence | Lit 12 Presentation |
|---|---|---|---|---|---|---|---|---|---|---|---|
| 1.1 | 2.1 | 3.1 | 4.1 | 5.1 | 6.1 | 7.1 | 8.1 | 9.1 | 10.1 | 11.1 | 12.1 |
| 1.2 | 2.2 | 3.2 | 4.2 | 5.2 | 6.2 | 7.2 | 8.2 | 9.2 | 10.2 | 11.2 | 12.2 |

## Numeracy

| Num 1 U&A | Num 2 Count | Num 3 Number | Num 4 Calculate | Num 5 Shape | Num 6 Measure | Num 7 Data |
|---|---|---|---|---|---|---|
| 1.1 | 2.1 | 3.1 | 4.1 | 5.1 | 6.1 | 7.1 |
| 1.2 | 2.2 | 3.2 | 4.2 | 5.2 | 6.2 | 7.2 |

## Science

| SC1 Enquiry | | | SC2 Life processes | | | | | SC3 Materials | | SC4 Physical processes | | |
|---|---|---|---|---|---|---|---|---|---|---|---|---|
| Sc 1.1 | Sc 1.2 | Sc 1.3 | Sc 2.1 | Sc 2.2 | Sc 2.3 | Sc 2.4 | Sc 2.5 | Sc 3.1 | Sc 3.2 | Sc 4.1 | Sc4.2 | Sc 4.3 |
| 1.1a | 1.2a | 1.3a | 2.1a | 2.2a | 2.3a | 2.4a | 2,5a | 3.1a | 3.2a | 4.1a | 4.2a | 4.3a |
| 1.1b | 1.2b | 1.3b | 2.1b | 2.2b | 2.3b | 2.4b | 2,5b | 3.1b | 3.2b | 4.1b | 4.2b | 4.3b |
| 1.1c | 1.2c | 1.3c | 2.1c | 2.2c | 2.3c | | 2,5c | 3.1c | | 4.1c | 4.2c | 4.3c |
| 1.1d | | | | 2.2d | | | | 3.1d | | | | 4.3d |
| | | | | 2.2e | | | | | | | | |
| | | | | 2.2f | | | | | | | | |
| | | | | 2.2g | | | | | | | | |

## Notes on how to take the learning forward

## History

| H1 Chronology | H2 Events, people | H3 Interpret | H4 Enquire | H5 Org and comm | H6 Breadth |
|---|---|---|---|---|---|
| 1a | 2a | 3a | 4a | 5a | 6a |
| 1b | 2b | | 4b | | 6b |
| | | | | 6c | |
| | | | | 6d | |

## Geography

| G1.1 and | G1.2 Enquiry | G2 Places | G3 Processes | G4 Environment | G5 Breadth |
|---|---|---|---|---|---|
| 1.1a | 1.2a | 2a | 3a | 4a | 5a |
| 1.1b | 1.2b | 2b | 3b | 4b | 5b |
| 1.1c | 1.2c | 2c | | | 5c |
| 1.1d | 1.2d | 2d | | | 5d |
| | | 2e | | | |

## Music

| M1 Performing | M2 Composing | M3 Appraising | M4 Listening | M5 Breadth |
|---|---|---|---|---|
| 1a | 2a | 3a | 4a | 5a |
| 1b | 2b | 3b | 4b | 5b |
| 1c | | | 4c | 5c |
| | | | 5d | |

## Art and Design

| A&D 1 Ideas | A&D 2 Making | A&D 3 Evaluating | A&D 4 Materials | A&D 5 Breadth |
|---|---|---|---|---|
| 1a | 2a | 3a | 4a | 5a |
| 1b | 2b | 3b | 4b | 5b |
| | 2c | | 4c | 5c |
| | | | | 5d |

## Design and Technology

| D&T 1 Developing | D&T 2 Tool use | D&T 3 Evaluating | D&T 4 Materials | D&T 5 Breadth |
|---|---|---|---|---|
| 1a | 2a | 3a | 4a | 5a |
| 1b | 2b | 3b | 4b | 5b |
| 1c | 2c | | | 5c |
| 1d | 2d | | | |
| 1e | 2e | | | |

## PSHE

| PSHE1 Confidence and respect | PSHE2 Citizenship | PSHE3 Health | PSHE4 Relationships |
|---|---|---|---|
| 1a | 2a | 3a | 4a |
| 1b | 2b | 3b | 4b |
| 1c | 2c | 3c | 4c |
| 1d | 2d | 3d | 4d |
| 1e | 2e | 3e | 4e |
| | 2f | 3f | |
| | 2g | 3g | |
| | 2h | | |

## ICT

| ICT1 Finding out | | ICT2 Ideas | ICT3 Reviewing | ICT4 Breadth |
|---|---|---|---|---|
| 1.1a | 1.2a | 2a | 3a | 4a |
| 1.1b | 1.2b | 2b | 3b | 4b |
| 1.1c | 1.2c | 2c | 3c | 4c |
| | 1.2d | | | |

## PE

| PE 1 Develop skills | PE 2 Apply skills | PE 3 Evaluate | PE 4 Fitness | PE 5 Breadth |
|---|---|---|---|---|
| 1a | 2a | 3a | 4a | 5a dance |
| 1b | 2b | 3b | 4b | 5b games |
| | 2c | 3c | | 5c gym |

| Critical skills | Thinking skills |
|---|---|
| problem solving | observing |
| decision making | classifying |
| critical thinking | prediction |
| creative thinking | making inferences |
| communication | problem solving |
| organisation | drawing conclusions |
| management | |
| leadership | |

# Clay

## Previous experience

Many settings use clay as an additional material, as it has properties unlike any other malleable material. However, some settings will have avoided it for various reasons. Those children who have had access to clay may have:

- used it in free play
- rolled coils for constructions
- used clay in role-play and home corner play as 'pretend' objects and food
- made simple models and shapes.

Others may not have had any experience of clay and may need encouragement to address its challenges as well as experiencing its unique properties.

## The responsive adult

In the early stages of working with clay it is crucial to continue to observe the children. Only by doing this can you set developmentally appropriate challenges and provocations. The ideas listed here are offered as suggestions; the most exciting challenges will arise from children's own interests and motivations, which will only become apparent as you spend time with them, watching and joining them in their play. As you do this, you will be moving between the three interconnecting roles of observer, co-player, extender described below, and will be able to decide what you need to do next to take the learning forward. In three interconnecting roles, the responsive adult will be:

### Observer

- observing
- listening
- interpreting

### Co-player

- modelling
- playing alongside
- offering suggestions
- responding sensitively
- initiating with care!

### Extender

- discussing ideas
- sharing thinking
- modelling new skills
- asking open questions
- being an informed extender
- instigating ideas and thoughts
- supporting children as they make links in learning
- making possibilities evident
- introducing new ideas and resources
- offering challenges and provocations

## Offering challenges and provocations

You may choose to use clay that does not need firing (e.g. Newclay) or potter's clay which either needs firing in a kiln or using it as it is but recognising its shortcomings. Painting any clay with PVA glue will lengthen its life, even though it may not prevent breaking. Whichever type you choose, children need periods of free play before addressing any challenges. Clay also needs to be kept damp!

- Can you use clay to make long 'sausages' or 'snakes'? Who can make the longest? Now coil your snakes and make them into flat mats or tiles. You can smooth out the joins or leave them as a decoration. What happens to your clay as it dries?

- Get some rolling pins and roll some clay until it is flat. Cut some squares or other shapes with a knife. Now decorate your clay tiles with patterns, pictures or writing, using old pencils, sticks or twigs from the garden.

- Some animals are good to make with clay — choose ones with shorter legs and fatter bodies, such as hedgehogs. Make a list of the animals you could try (use a book or Google to help you). Now make some animals from the list — use tools such as pencils or scissors to make fur and feather patterns, or stick on natural materials such as feathers or leaves. When your animals are finished, you could fire them in a kiln, or cover them with a layer of PVA glue.

- Use some flat clay to take prints. Roll the clay out, press natural objects into the surface, leave the clay for a while, then paint the surface. How can you turn this into a print on paper or fabric?

- Make some very runny clay by adding lots of water and stirring it up. Use this clay as paint or ink to draw or write on paper with paint brushes. What happens if you paint all over the paper and leave it to dry? How could you use it now?

## Ready for more?

◆ Try doing some cave paintings. Get some clay and make it very runny by mixing with water. Put it in several pots and colour the different pots with some of these natural dyes:

- turmeric (a yellow spice)
- blackberry or blueberry juice
- charcoal or soot

Now use your paints to paint on card, paper, or even a wall. Look at the great images of cave paintings on Google Images 'cave paintings'.

◆ Use clay to make hand prints. Make blocks as big as your hand and press your hand into the block. Get your friends to do the same. What do you find out?

◆ Make lots of balls of clay. Can you use these to make a sculpture?

◆ Get some wire netting. Make it into a structure and cover it with clay. How did you do it?

◆ Look up 'terracotta army' in Google Images. These soldiers were found in China. Can you find out how many there are? Could you make a terracotta soldier?

◆ Use Google Images to find pictures of terracotta sculptures of your favourite animals. Why is this sort of sculpture called terracotta? How do you cook clay?

# Materials, websites, books and other references

## Materials

Clay is a cheap and versatile natural material. There are lots of different sorts, and you may want to offer a choice of types or colours:

- grey or buff clay is school standard, clean and easy to use. Get this from your school supplier or consortium

- terracotta or red clay is the most authentic, but it does stain hands and other surfaces

- Newclay or self-hardening clay is useful as the fibres within the clay can be hardened with a special hardener, so creations don't need firing — see http://www.newclay.co.uk/Products.htm for newclay products and other clays

- If you live or work on clay soil, you could help the children to dig their own clay direct from the ground!

## Ideas

Visit your local museum or art gallery, or look online for sculptors and potters in your area who may be prepared to visit you or open their studio for a visit.

## Google images

For inspiration for creation type in
- sculpture
- clay model
- animal sculpture
- cat sculpture (or any animal).

## Books

There are hundreds of books on using clay and making sculptures. Here are just a few books for younger readers:

**Fun with Modeling Clay**; Barbara Reid; Kids Can Press

**Ceramics for Kids**; Mary Ellis; Lark Books

**Clay in the Primary School**; Peter Clough; A&C Black

**The Great Clay Adventure: Creative Handbuilding Projects for Young Artists**; Ellen Kong; Davis Publications

**Children, Clay and Sculpture**; Cathy Weisman Topal; Davis Publications

**Exploring Clay with Children: 20 Simple Projects**; Chris Utley; A&C Black

## Websites

www.commotionstore.co.uk - for clay tools

www.warriortours.com/.../xian/0010656.htm - to look at the Terracotta army

http://www.schoolsliaison.org.uk/kids/greecepot.htm Birmingham Museum children's site

http://www.gladstone.stoke.gov.uk/ccm/portal/ Stoke on Trent Museum service for visits to the Potteries.

'museum pottery kids' in a search engine such as google will find lots of museums with facilities for schools.

# Mud and compost

## Previous experience

Mud and compost are free resources for all schools, and are now a feature of most early years settings. The majority of children will have experimented with and explored these resources in:

- making mud pies
- working with mud in a builder's tray, with diggers, small world figures and vehicles
- making miniature gardens
- playing in a digging area, with and without tools, burying objects in mud and digging them up again
- planting and gardening in pots and in the ground
- paddling in muddy puddles
- mixing water with mud for painting.

## The responsive adult

In the early stages of working with these materials it is crucial to continue to observe the children. Only by doing this can you set developmentally appropriate challenges and provocations. The ideas listed here are offered as suggestions; the most exciting challenges will arise from children's own interests and motivations, which will only become apparent as you spend time with them, watching and joining them in their play. As you do this, you will be moving between the three interconnecting roles of observer, co-player, extender described below, and will be able to decide what you need to do next to take the learning forward. In three interconnecting roles, the responsive adult will be:

### Observer

- observing
- listening
- interpreting

### Co-player

- modelling
- playing alongside
- offering suggestions
- responding sensitively
- initiating with care!

### Extender

- discussing ideas
- sharing thinking
- modelling new skills
- asking open questions
- being an informed extender
- instigating ideas and thoughts
- supporting children as they make links in learning
- making possibilities evident
- introducing new ideas and resources
- offering challenges and provocations

## Offering challenges and provocations

Some children (and adults) need to get used to using mud and compost. If the children are not used to these media, give them time to experiment.

- Can you find some mud that can be easily moulded? Try digging mud from different places to see which is most malleable.
- Can you change the colour of mud by adding different substances to it, for example, powder, ready-mixed paint or food colouring?
- Can you change the consistency of mud by adding things like water, wallpaper paste, sand or flour?
- Can you make a castle, or other type of building from mud? What could you use to make turrets and towers? Can you make bridges from mud?
- Make a cave from mud, and use some small world fantasy characters to make stories and plays.
- Can you create a habitat for small world animals?
- Can you construct some bowls and find ways of drying them out so that they do not break? Can you stop them breaking by mixing other things with the mud?

- Can you make your own bricks and then design some buildings that you could make using them?
- Can you make a tunnel with mud? Who can make the longest tunnel? Can you find ways of reinforcing your tunnel to make it stronger?
- How could you make a sculpture of a person or animal from mud? Which animals are easy to make? Is it harder to make a person sculpture or an animal sculpture?
- Can you make some decorative mud pies? How many different materials can you find for decorating them, for example, flowers, feathers, leaves, shells and stones?
- Take photographs of your mud pies and use them to make a decorative picture, book or wall hanging.

## Ready for more?

♦ Google 'mud sculptures' to see if you can find different ways of working with mud.

♦ Can you make a mythical beast, dragon or similar creature? You may need to use other materials such as twigs or sticks to help support your sculpture.

♦ Can you combine other materials with mud, for example, straw or newspaper to make 'cob' houses or other structures? Look on Google Images for 'cob cottages' for some information.

♦ Make some mud casts of handprints, footprints and other objects which leave impressions in mud. Once they are dry, fill them with plaster of Paris. Look for some footprints or animal prints around the school grounds or gardens. Try making mud casts of these and finding out what made them.

♦ Can you create a 'living sculpture' by adding seeds and plants to your sculpture? For example, sow grass seeds to make 'hair' or mustard and cress seeds for fur.

♦ Try making some tiles with your mud, by flattening it and cutting the tiles out. Look for some pictures of mosaics and decorate or colour your tiles to make your own mosaic?

♦ Experiment with sieves and colanders to strain the water.

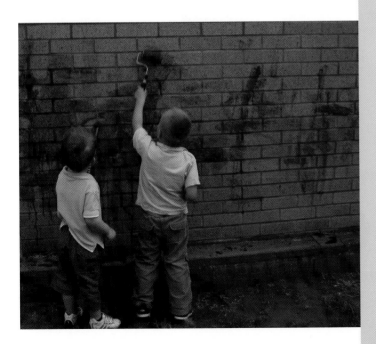

# Materials, websites, books and other references

## Materials

Mud is free, but if children are going to use their hands, **it should be collected from places where it has not been fouled by animals**. If you don't have access to clean earth, buy a bag of compost from a garden centre.

Any tools will do for work with mud:

■ small sized gardening tools

■ old spoons, forks and blunt knives

■ yogurt pots and other recycled materials

■ sticks, twigs and other found objects.

## Google images

For inspiration for creation type in:

• **mud sculpture** for a great hippo sculpture

• **mud sculpture kids**

• **cob cottage** for buildings covered in mud

• **mud bricks**.

## Websites

http://www.pbase.com/qleap/mud for some great pictures of children in the Arizona Mud Mania. Go to the home page and click on each year for a gallery of photos.

Google searching **fun with mud** will give you lots of sites with mud races and mud festivals.

**I am Clay** is an American DVD for teachers about the benefits of clay work. Watch a preview with some good ideas, or order the video on http://k-play.com/I_am_clay.html - there is a gallery on the same site with examples of children's work from a range of ages.

http://www.iamanartist.ie/clay/ has a slide show and lots of ideas - just click on the drawings.

## Books

Some suitable books for younger readers include:

**Mudworks**; MaryAnn F. Kohl; Bright Ring Publishing

**Mud Pies and Other Recipes: A Cookbook for Dolls**; Marjorie Winslow; Walker & Company

**Mud Pie Annie**; Sue Buchanan; ZonderKidz

**Stuck in the Mud**; Jane Clarke; Puffin Books

**Making Art with Sand and Earth**; Gillian Chapman; PowerKids Press

**Let's Make Mud!** Gwenda Turner; Penguin Books NZ

**Mud, Grass, and Ice Homes** (Homes Around the World); Debbie Gallagher; Smart Apple Media

**Mud Puddle**; Robert N. Munsch; Annick Press

**The Mud Monster**; Rosemary Billam; Franklin Watts

**Stuck in the Mud**; Shirley Jackson; Ladybird

# Dough

## Previous experience

By the time children leave the Foundation Stage they should have had wide experience of using dough in projects and particularly in free play:

- indoors and out of doors
- to make role-play objects
- with small world animals and figures
- to explore pattern and shape in three dimensions
- for strengthening hands and fingers
- exploring dough mixed with sand, glitter, perfumed oils and other substances
- to make models and familiar objects.

They should also have had experience of:

- working on specific projects with dough in language and mathematical activities.

## The responsive adult

In the early stages of working with these materials it is crucial to continue to observe the children. Only by doing this can you set developmentally appropriate challenges and provocations. The ideas listed here are offered as suggestions; the most exciting challenges will arise from children's own interests and motivations, which will only become apparent as you spend time with them, watching and joining them in their play. As you do this, you will be moving between the three interconnecting roles of observer, co-player, extender described below, and will be able to decide what you need to do next to take the learning forward. In three interconnecting roles, the responsive adult will be:

### Observer

- observing
- listening
- interpreting

### Co-player

- modelling
- playing alongside
- offering suggestions
- responding sensitively
- initiating with care!

### Extender

- discussing ideas
- sharing thinking
- modelling new skills
- asking open questions
- being an informed extender
- instigating ideas and thoughts
- supporting children as they make links in learning
- making possibilities evident
- introducing new ideas and resources
- offering challenges and provocations

## Offering challenges and provocations

It is important to find out the breadth of experience children have had during the Foundation Stage, particularly in using dough for projects. You may also want to explore making your own dough with the children.

- Get a copy of *The Little Book of Dough* (from Featherstone Education). This book has a huge range of recipes for making dough, using different sorts of materials and additions.

- Try making your own dough, using the *Little Book* or a recipe from the Internet. Find out what this dough can do, and take some photos.

- Can you make coloured dough? What could you use? You could try natural colourings like beetroot juice, onion skins or grated carrot.

- Can you make perfumed dough? What could you use? Look for food flavourings as well as perfumes.

- Can you make a big structure with dough? Try making lots of balls and using these to build with. Can you make a tower? A bridge? A wall?

- Make some dough that can be hardened in the oven or on a radiator. Roll some out and use objects to press in and make patterns on the dough. Make a hole with a pencil, so you can hang your decoration up. Wait until your decorations are dry, colour them with pens or paint, or just paint them with a mixture of white glue and water to stop them breaking.

- Make some edible dough and use this to make shaped or decorative biscuits or cookies, or decorate them with edible decorations when they are cooked. You could sell your biscuits to other children or take them home for your family to eat.

## Ready for more?

◆ Make some dough and colour it if you like. Use the dough to make bricks, then bake these until they are hard. Use your bricks to make structures and buildings. You can stick them together with glue, clay or uncooked dough.

◆ Use the internet, cookery books and craft books to make two lists of all the things you can use to make dough. You could list edible/not edible, cooked/not cooked, easy/difficult, cheap/expensive. Now choose some ingredients to make some dough yourself.

◆ Can you think of any more ingredients that you could use to make dough? Try some. Did it work?

◆ Make some dough that can be hardened in an oven. Colour it if you like, then use this dough to make some badges or fridge magnets. Roll the dough out and cut out small shapes. Decorate these with letters, marks, patterns, or press small objects into them (make sure these can be baked!). Bake the shapes on a baking sheet, then paint or colour them. Stick a magnet or a badge pin on the back. You could make these for your friends.

◆ Find out how to make dough from cotton wool or the fluff from tumble driers. Make some and see what it is like. Can you make dough with coffee, couscous, mashed potato, chocolate or sand?

# Materials, websites, books and other references

## Materials

There are hundreds of different recipes for dough, and many can be made by the children independently. Put 'dough recipe' in a search engine to come up with lots of ideas. Look on USA and worldwide sites as well, as these sometimes have unusual versions. Ask your local shops for flour that is past its 'sell by date' to use in dough recipes.

Educational suppliers all have a range of tools and other equipment for dough work - try www.tts-group.co.uk www.ascoeducational.co.uk or your local consortium group.

Look in Bargain and 'pound' shops for cutters and shaping tools, and encourage children to be inventive in the tools they make and the objects they use.

## Google images

To see lots of lovely pictures of dough creations search

- dough
- dough sculpture
- dough sculpture kids
- playdough
- kids dough
- salt dough
- dough recipes.

## Websites

http://www.multihobbies.com/saltdough/ has dough recipe and a gallery of dough creations.

## Books

Some suitable books for younger readers include:

**Salt Dough Models**; Sue Organ; Search Press

**The Little Book of Dough**; Lynn Garner; Featherstone Education

**Salt Dough**; Laura Torres; American Girl

**Salt Dough Fun**; Brigitte Casagranda; Gareth Stevens

# Wire

## Previous experience

Some settings are quite adventurous in offering children wire to work with. However, many children will have limited experience of working with wire, although they may have:

- experimented with pipe cleaners

- worked with an artist or practitioner to make things from chicken wire. They might have helped to add clay, plaster of paris or paper to wire to form a variety of shapes

- woven ribbon or other material through wire of different sorts

- used wire to make mobiles and hangings

N.B. Before allowing the children to work with wire be sure to spend time checking that they know how to do this safely!

## The responsive adult

In the early stages of working with these materials it is crucial to continue to observe the children. Only by doing this can you set developmentally appropriate challenges and provocations. The ideas listed here are offered as suggestions; the most exciting challenges will arise from children's own interests and motivations, which will only become apparent as you spend time with them, watching and joining them in their play. As you do this, you will be moving between the three interconnecting roles of observer, co-player, extender described below, and will be able to decide what you need to do next to take the learning forward. In three interconnecting roles, the responsive adult will be:

### Observer

- observing
- listening
- interpreting

### Co-player

- modelling
- playing alongside
- offering suggestions
- responding sensitively
- initiating with care!

### Extender

- discussing ideas
- sharing thinking
- modelling new skills
- asking open questions
- being an informed extender
- instigating ideas and thoughts
- supporting children as they make links in learning
- making possibilities evident
- introducing new ideas and resources
- offering challenges and provocations

## Offering challenges and provocations

Try to make wire available for construction and creative projects. Have clear rules and start with small lengths of plastic covered wire or pipe cleaners. Children need to be shown how to bend and shape the wire, and to cut it with wire snips.

- Can you design some jewellery and then make it by bending, twisting and decorating your wire? Can you make crowns, bracelets and necklaces? Can you add beads and sequins?

- Can you design and make some hanging decorations for the classroom and the outdoor area?

- Find out all you can about Dream Catchers and see if you can make some.

- Can you make some garden sculptures and incorporate twigs, leaves and bark into your designs?

- Google 'wire sculptures'. Use what you find as inspiration for some work of your own.

- Can you bend some wire to make interesting shapes and then cover it with papier mache?

- Google 'Anthony Gormley'. Look at some of the ways he uses wire to make sculptures. See if this gives you ideas for sculptures of your own.

- Can you work as a group or a class to make a large animal, person or mythical creature from wire, coat hangers, wire netting and other sorts of wire? Collect lots of different sorts of wire before you start, and work out of doors if you can. Decorate your wire sculpture with metal objects such as ring pulls from cans, foil, metal cases from food items such as jam tarts, bits of chain, washers, nuts and bolts. Fix the decorations with fuse wire — it's easier to manage.

## Ready for more?

♦ Can you make a sculpture that uses several different types of wire? You could collect fuse wire, plastic coated wire, coat hangers, green garden wire, cable, jeweller's wire, curtain wire and wire netting - there are hundreds of different sorts!

♦ Can you twist wire to make a variety of three dimensional shapes? Hang these up to make a mathematical mobile.

♦ Can you 'write' your name in wire? Put 'wire name' in Google Images for some ideas of how to do it.

♦ Now can you work as a group or a class to 'write' a short verse in wire?

♦ Can you make a den by wiring twigs and branches together and covering your shelter with plastic sheet or thin fabric?

♦ Can you use wire to make a house for a toy or a garage for a car? How could you make this waterproof?

♦ Look a www.nshima.com/2008/05/the-creativeki. html to find information about some boys in Zimbabwe who make cars from wire.

♦ Can you use wire to make a boat? Can you make it waterproof and find a way to make it float?

♦ Can you think of other materials that could be combined with wire to make structures and sculptures, for example, rolled up newspaper or cardboard?

## Materials

The following sorts of wire are suitable for children to use. You may need to provide some adult help with some, but with care and training, children can work competently to produce wire creations.

■ soldering wire is very soft and can be easily bent by hand;

■ picture hanging wire comes in gold and silver;

■ jewellery wire can be purchased on line from hundreds of craft sites;

■ electrical cable can be stripped of its outer casing to reveal several strands of plastic covered wire;

■ wire coat hangers are very useful for making mobiles and hanging creations;

■ wire netting is great for making big sculptures;

■ plastic bag ties are safe and cheap;

■ copper wire is easily formed round simple objects.

Offer children plenty of other objects to add to their creations - beads, feathers, sequins, tape, ribbon pieces, fabric scraps, coloured paper, old pieces of jewellery etc.

Simple tools, such as wire snips, pliers, silversmithing tools all come in small sizes suitable for children to choose. They also help with winding wire round objects to make spirals and other shapes.

## Google images

For inspiration for creation type in:

• wire sculpture

• wire structure

• wire sculpture reggio

• wire sculpture

• wire sculpture kids

# Materials, websites, books and other references

## Websites

http://www.whiteoakschool.com/reggio-resources/ for Reggio Emilia resources and magazines

wire artists http://www.vistagallery.com/html/sten_hoiland. html or www.yessy.com - and look for the work of Michael Wilcox

The following websites have articles about some African children who make cars from recycled wire:

www.nshima.com/2008/05/the-creative-ki.html or

http://www.highlightskids.com/science/stories/SS1105_wirecars.asp

http://www.wire-magic.co.uk/gallery.html is a gallery full of images of wires sculptures form all sorts of artists - certainly worth exploring with the children.

## Books

Rush on Paper: An Introduction to Modelling Wire and Paper Figures; Peter Rush; James Hockey Gallery

# Paper pulp

## Previous experience

Paper is a free resource, and many children will have played with shreddings and torn paper. Some will have made papier maché with strips of sheets of paper to make:

- models
- scenes for small world play
- bowls and small plates
- coverings for pots and tubs
- covering balloons for instruments and puppet heads.

These activities may have evolved around:

- stories and poems
- puppet play
- seasonal themes and gift making
- themes from nature

and been inspired by art work from a wide range of cultures.

## The responsive adult

In the early stages of working with these materials it is crucial to continue to observe the children. Only by doing this can you set developmentally appropriate challenges and provocations. The ideas listed here are offered as suggestions; the most exciting challenges will arise from children's own interests and motivations, which will only become apparent as you spend time with them, watching and joining them in their play. As you do this, you will be moving between the three interconnecting roles of observer, co-player, extender described below, and will be able to decide what you need to do next to take the learning forward. In three interconnecting roles, the responsive adult will be:

## Observer

- observing
- listening
- interpreting

## Co-player

- modelling
- playing alongside
- offering suggestions
- responding sensitively
- initiating with care!

## Extender

- discussing ideas
- sharing thinking
- modelling new skills
- asking open questions
- being an informed extender
- instigating ideas and thoughts
- supporting children as they make links in learning
- making possibilities evident
- introducing new ideas and resources
- offering challenges and provocations

## Offering challenges and provocations

Recycled paper is a free resource which is ideal for this activity. Shreddings from a shredder, scrap paper, newspaper or junk mail can also be used. Avoid very shiny paper from magazines, and be aware that the print will affect the colour of the pulp, and may colour children's hands!

- Collect some scrap paper and tear it into very small pieces. Add some cellulose paste and water to make a sloshy mixture. Stir it with a stick or your hand, squeezing the paper so it dissolves in the liquid. Keep stirring for a day until the pulp is well mixed and the paper is soaked right through, but not too wet. If it is too runny, add some more paper.

- The next day, tip some of the paper pulp on to a board or table top, and squeeze it with your hands. Keep squishing till the paper pulp is smooth. Now use your hands to mould the pulp into a shape. Watch and feel how it behaves in your hands. Can you build tall structures?

- Use some of your pulp to make a bowl or cup. You may need to squeeze some of the water out with your hands before you start. When you have made your cup or bowl, leave it somewhere warm to dry. It may take several days to dry right through - putting it near a radiator or in a VERY low oven will speed up the process. Microwaving doesn't work.

- Use something as a shaper or former for your paper pulp - you could use small bowls, yogurt pots, plant pots or anything with a smooth surface. Turn the shaper upside down and put pulp all over it. Smooth the pulp with your hands, or leave it rough, whichever you wish. When the pulp is dry, you should be able to remove the shaper. What does the inside of your creation feel like? Is it the same as the outside?

- Try some different shapers and decorate them with paint, felt pens, beads, sequins and other small objects.

## Ready for more?

◆ Do an experiment. Make pulp with different sorts of paper. Try:

- shiny magazine paper
- crepe or tissue paper
- paper towels
- tissues or kitchen roll
- newspaper.

Which works best - which is the least successful?

◆ Work as a class. Collect newspapers from everyone you know, and make a huge amount of pulp in buckets. Now get a big sheet of wood or strong card and use your paper pulp to make a landscape. You could make:

- a moon or space scene
- a historic scene;
- high mountains
- a fantasy landscape.
- a model of your school or your area.

◆ Dont forget to take photos! Remember that paper pulp takes a long time to dry, so be patient! When it is dry you could paint the landscape. What could you use for trees? For roads or streets? For buildings? For castles and caves? For rivers and lakes? Can you find or make some people the right scale or size for your landscape? Find some wire netting and see if you can make a big sculpture using wire netting and lots of paper pulp.

# Materials, websites, books and other references

## Materials

Any sort of paper can be used for sculptures and creations. Newspaper and other 'pulpy' papers are best for making papier mache or paper pulp - avoid shiny magazine paper - it doesn't soak up the paste well. Collect paper that can be recycled into pulp, and add some texture and colouring e.g.

- crepe paper to colour pulp
- sand, sawdust or compost to add texture
- seeds of all sorts such as grass seed, melon or sunflower seeds
- herbs and spices for texture and perfume
- aromatherapy oils
- paint or food colouring
- glitter or sequins.

## Google Images

For images of paper sculpture and other work, type in:

- paper sculpture
- papier mâché sculpture
- paper weaving
- paper craft.

## Books

Some suitable books to use with younger children include:

**Papier-mâché for Kids**; Sheila McGraw; Firefly Books

**Art Attack: How to Papier Mâché**; Karen Brown; Panini

**Papier Mâché**; Ray Gibson; Usborne

**Creating with Papier Mâché**; Victoria Seix; Blackbirch Press

**Papier Mâché**; Design Eye Publishing

**Papier Mâché**; Judy Balchin; Search Press

**Decorative Painting**; Judy Balchin; Search Press

**Spectacular Paper Sculptures**; Ron Van Der Meer; Robin Corey Books

**Complete Book of Paper Mask Making**; Michael Grater; Dover Pubs

**Paper, Scissors, Sculpt!: Creating Cut-and-fold Animals**; Ben A. Gonzales; Sterling Juvenile

**Mobiles and Other Paper Wind Catchers**; Phyllis Fiarotta; Sterling

**Look What You Can Make with Tubes**; Margie Hayes Richmond; Boyds Mills Press

**Look What You Can Make from Paper Plates**; Margie Hayes Richmond; Boyds Mills Press

**Look What You Can Make with Newspapers, Magazines, and Greeting Cards**; Kathy Ross; Boyds Mills Press

**Look What You Can Make with Plastic Bottles and Tubs**; Kathy Ross; Boyds Mills Press

# Ice

## Previous experience

Exploring and experimenting with ice is a common activity in early year's settings so most children will have some experience of the properties of ice in one form or another. They may have:

- played with ice as part of water play
- eaten ice lollies
- observed icicles and frozen puddles in the winter
- carried out experiments with ice
- made ice shapes in the freezer in containers of different sorts and sizes.

## The responsive adult

In the early stages of working with these materials it is crucial to continue to observe the children. Only by doing this can you set developmentally appropriate challenges and provocations. The ideas listed here are offered as suggestions; the most exciting challenges will arise from children's own interests and motivations, which will only become apparent as you spend time with them, watching and joining them in their play. As you do this, you will be moving between the three interconnecting roles of observer, co-player, extender described below, and will be able to decide what you need to do next to take the learning forward. In three interconnecting roles, the responsive adult will be:

### Observer

- observing
- listening
- interpreting

### Co-player

- modelling
- playing alongside
- offering suggestions
- responding sensitively
- initiating with care!

### Extender

- discussing ideas
- sharing thinking
- modelling new skills
- asking open questions
- being an informed extender
- instigating ideas and thoughts
- supporting children as they make links in learning
- making possibilities evident
- introducing new ideas and resources
- offering challenges and provocations

## Offering challenges and provocations

- Make a collection of interesting cartons and containers that could be used to freeze water in. You should be able to find lots of recycled containers, but think of some more unusual ones too. You can try anything that doesn't leak!

- Can you make some moulds of your own with plasticine and freeze water in these?

- Can you design some fruit slushes for your friends to try? How many different flavours can you create?

- Can you design a range of ice lollies using different flavours of fruit juice?

- How many different shapes can you make?
  - How many different flavours?
  - How many different colours?

- Can you think of ways to make a multi-coloured ice lolly? How did you do it?

- What is the largest block of ice you can create? Try all sorts of containers.

- Can you create an ice-sculpture by chipping bits from a large block of ice? NB. Remember to wear goggles to protect your eyes!

- Try freezing objects into blocks of ice, for example a key. How long do you think it will take to get the key out?

- Can you write a story about the frozen key, how it got frozen and what happened to it next?

- Get a lot of ice cubes (you can buy a bag from a supermarket) and see if you can make the cubes into a sculpture.

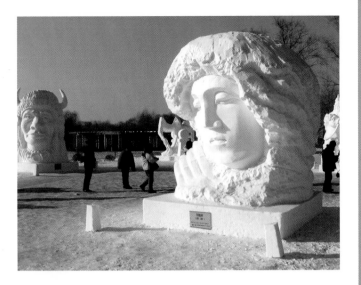

## Ready for more?

◆ Try freezing flowers into ice cubes. Make arrangements with your frozen ice cubes and photograph them to make cards, pictures, book marks and other designs.

◆ Experiment with plastic bags and string. Put some water into the bag. Tie it off with string and then add more water to make some interesting shapes.

◆ Use frozen blocks and ice cubes to make a structure for some small world arctic characters. Can you build a frozen environment for small world polar bears, penguins and other arctic creatures?

◆ Hold some competitions with your friends to see who can get a block of ice to melt the fastest. Try different ways and make a graph of the results.

◆ Hold some competitions to see who can keep a block of ice frozen for the longest period of time. What are the best insulators?

◆ Freeze string into ice cubes so that you can use them to make mobiles and decorations to hang outside.

◆ In winter, go on an ice hunt and make the ice into mobiles and other decorations.

◆ Google 'ice sculptures' and 'ice hotel'. See if you can find new ideas for ice sculptures.

◆ Make some ice balloons by filling balloons with water. Freeze interesting things inside like glitter or tinsel.

## Materials

Making ice is a cheap and interesting activity if you have a freezer at school or are prepared to use your own at home. Encourage the children to be adventurous in the moulds they use and the way they use the ice for constructions. Try some of these:

■ recycled containers such as yogurt pots, plastic bottles

■ the liners from chocolates, sweet boxes, or food trays

■ unusual items such as plastic or rubber gloves

■ balloons with or without small objects inside

■ big containers such as ice cream tubs.

If you don't have easy access to a freezer, you can do a lot of interesting activities with bags of ice cubes form a freezer centre or a supermarket. Some children may like to work with gloves. Collect interesting items to freeze in the ice - these can include:

■ small toys;

■ beads, sequins, seeds;

■ leaves, flowers, petals, grass.

## Google images

• ice festival        • ice cube flower

## Websites

http://www.grandeurice.com/ and click on 'gallery' for ice sculptures

http://www.bbc.co.uk/norfolk/content/image_galleries/ events_ice_sculpture_20071216_gallery.shtml for images of an ice sculpture trail

www.icesculpture.co.uk/ for more images, and for instructions for a glowing ice ball - http:// portlandoregonweddingphotographer. wordpress. com/2008/05/19/how-to-make-a-glowing-ice-ball/ a video.

## Books

Midsummer Snowballs; Andy Goldsworthy; Thames & Hudson is a book about the huge snowballs that the artist placed around London one summer. He had frozen snow during the winter and then left them out in June! See the report on http://news.bbc.co.uk/1/hi/uk/800916.stm or put 'goldsworthy snowballs' in Google Images to see the snowballs and some other ice sculptures he has made.

# Plaster and plaster bandages

## Previous experience

Children may never have used plaster or plaster bandages before. If they have, it will probably be in supervised activities such as:

- making hand or foot prints

- wrapping simple objects with plaster bandage.

Plaster of Paris is a complex and difficult material to use. It dries very quickly and doesn't re-constitute if you add water. It is also fairly expensive for free use.

However it does have unique properties which older children can fruitfully explore, making and discussing scientific observations, learning about the properties of materials and investigating change.

## The responsive adult

In the early stages of working with these materials it is crucial to continue to observe the children. Only by doing this can you set developmentally appropriate challenges and provocations. The ideas listed here are offered as suggestions; the most exciting challenges will arise from children's own interests and motivations, which will only become apparent as you spend time with them, watching and joining them in their play. As you do this, you will be moving between the three interconnecting roles of observer, co-player, extender described below, and will be able to decide what you need to do next to take the learning forward. In three interconnecting roles, the responsive adult will be:

### Observer

- observing
- listening
- interpreting

### Co-player

- modelling
- playing alongside
- offering suggestions
- responding sensitively
- initiating with care!

### Extender

- discussing ideas
- sharing thinking
- modelling new skills
- asking open questions
- being an informed extender
- instigating ideas and thoughts
- supporting children as they make links in learning
- making possibilities evident
- introducing new ideas and resources
- offering challenges and provocations

## Offering challenges and provocations

Plaster of Paris is a useful substance for exploring how materials change and those which cannot be returned to their original form. Plaster needs careful supervision because the methods are crucial. However, plaster bandage is a fascinating resource which children will love to use in constructing sculptures and objects.

- Work in a group to explore some Plaster of Paris. Find some small containers, put some small objects in the bottom of them and pour a mixture of plaster and water into the pots. Hold the pots. Can you feel anything? Watch the plaster - what is happening? When the plaster is dry tip it out of the pot and see what has happened to the objects you put in the bottom?

- Use this method to make some bird cakes with plaster and bird seed. How can you do it? Do the birds like their cakes? Take some photos of which birds come to your food.

- Now can you think of some other ways to use the plaster of Paris to make casts and patterns?

- Find some plaster bandage (called Modroc) and read the instructions. How could you use the plaster bandage to:

  - make a cast of your hand or foot;

  - make structures by putting it over things?

- Look outside for some footprints or other marks in the mud or soil. Can you use plaster of Paris to make casts of these prints? Remember that plaster sets very quickly, so you will have to work fast!

- Find some sticks and twigs. Set the twigs in small pots of plaster and decorate them. You could use beads, sequins, glitter, ribbon, or 'found objects' such as leaves, shells, bark or moss.

## Ready for more?

♦ Make a bigger version of the twig sculpture using a larger branch and working as a group. You could spray or paint the branch and decorate it for a festival. If you dip Modroc bandages in water and lay them flat to dry, you can cut them into lacy decorations which you can spray and hang on your branch.

♦ Find out about the Invisible Man, and why he had to wrap his head in bandages. Can you make an invisible man model using a small world figure? Make up a story about him, and take some photos for a display, a book or a PowerPoint presentation.

♦ Find out about Anthony Gormley who makes sculptures from his own body by wrapping it in bandages. Can you use a small world toy or superhero model to make a sculpture with plaster bandages?

♦ Collect some recycled materials and use these with plaster bandages to make some abstract sculptures. Look on **http://artseducation. suite101.com/article. cfm/plaster_bandage_s culptures** for help in doing this. You could work together to make something big for your playground or garden. If you want to make an outdoor sculpture, use outdoor paint to protect it from the weather.

♦ Can you think of a way to make a mask from plaster bandage?

# Materials, websites, books and other references

## Materials

Get Modroc bandage from:

**www.craftmill.co.uk** - modroc bandages and sheets, air drying clay, tools, shaped cutters

**http://www.modroc.com/modroctips.htm** - great tips for using modroc

**http://www.accessart.org.uk/modroc.php** - how to use modroc

**www.tts-group.co.uk** - for modroc and plaster of paris, newclay, tools, rollers, rolling pins, buff and red clay.

You can get casting plaster from chemists and from specialist craft shops and websites.

## Ideas

Find out how to make plaster casts on these sites:

**www.wildyorkshire.co.uk/naturediary/docs/2003/5/5.html** footprints in the mud, and

**www.rspb.org.uk/youth/makeanddo/activities/tracks. asp** for a download of a simple guide to the footprints of common birds and animals.

## Websites

For guidance on making landscapes, look at sites for model railway enthusiasts or architects.

**http://fun.familyeducation.com/childrens-art-activities/ sculpting/40287.html** has an activity called plaster box etching.

## Books

Let's Model with Plaster; Eileen Geipel; Evans Bros

## Google Images

- footprints plaster
- plaster casting
- plaster cast head
- plaster cast hand
- plaster foot

# Balsa wood and sandpaper

## Previous experience

Balsa wood is sometimes used in the EYFS for simple woodwork projects as it is soft and easily worked. Children may have:

- seen and worked with balsa wood

- used sandpaper as part of woodworking play

- seen balsa wood in models and constructions.

However, these materials - both sandpaper and balsa wood will be new and unfamiliar, needing time for free exploration

## The responsive adult

In the early stages of working with these materials it is crucial to continue to observe the children. Only by doing this can you set developmentally appropriate challenges and provocations. The ideas listed here are offered as suggestions; the most exciting challenges will arise from children's own interests and motivations, which will only become apparent as you spend time with them, watching and joining them in their play. As you do this, you will be moving between the three interconnecting roles of observer, co-player, extender described below, and will be able to decide what you need to do next to take the learning forward. In three interconnecting roles, the responsive adult will be:

### Observer

- observing
- listening
- interpreting

### Co-player

- modelling
- playing alongside
- offering suggestions
- responding sensitively
- initiating with care!

### Extender

- discussing ideas
- sharing thinking
- modelling new skills
- asking open questions
- being an informed extender
- instigating ideas and thoughts
- supporting children as they make links in learning
- making possibilities evident
- introducing new ideas and resources
- offering challenges and provocations

## Offering challenges and provocations

If balsa is an entirely new material for many children, it is really important that they have time to explore and experiment to find out about its properties. Start with some quite thick pieces of wood and some sandpaper or sanding blocks and spend some time discussing what happens and the children's observations on the activity. You may wish to focus on:

- how the wood feels

- how children think it might be different from other types of wood

- what they think it is used for

- the children's own ideas for how they think they could use it.

It may also be useful so show the children how thin balsa wood can be cut with scissors and glued with PVA glue.

- Can you make a boat from a piece of balsa wood, using just sandpaper to shape it? Will it float? Can you make it sink? How did you do this?

- Can your balsa wood boat carry anything - for example, a play person or a small world animal?

- Can you make some jewellery from balsa wood, for example, a pendant, a badge or a brooch? How could you colour the wood?

- Can you find ways of making a hole in a piece of balsa wood?

- Can you make a wood block to use for printing?

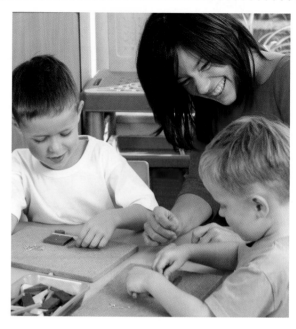

- Can you make some furniture for a doll's house by sticking and sanding balsa wood?

- Can you make a castle for some kings, queens and knights?

- Can you create a balsa wood design that you can take rubbings from?

- Can you make your name from balsa wood?

## Ready for more?

♦ Can you make a mythical beast or fantasy figure from balsa wood? You could make the figure flat, so it could play a part in a shadow play or an OHP projection.

♦ Balsa wood is good for making scenery and environments for plays and stories. Can you make some scenery for the fantasy figure to inhabit? Put 'balsa wood model' in Google Images to see some buildings and other models.

♦ Can you add other materials to make the habitat for your creature more interesting and exciting?

♦ Can you build a 'set' for a story, for example, *Little Red Riding Hood* or *Goldilocks and the Three Bears*?

♦ Can you build a balsa wood tower?

♦ Can you make a balsa wood plane or glider? Will it fly? Look on Google Images 'balsa wood plane' for some ideas.

♦ Can you make a wild and wonderful bird from balsa wood? Find some feathers to decorate your bird. You could hang it up or even see if it will fly.

♦ Can you write an information book on the uses of balsa wood?

♦ Can you write instructions for how to make a balsa wood model such as a plane or a bird? You could take photos as you make one or even get your friend to make a video of you doing it.

# Materials, websites, books and other references

## Materials

It's better to get balsa wood from educational or craft suppliers such as **www.tts-group.co.uk** who supply balsa wood in packs.

Try DIY superstores and bargain shops for sandpaper in bulk.

Get several different grades for finer or rougher finishes. Use wooden bricks or small wooden offcuts to make sanding blocks, or buy sponge sanding blocks from DIY shops.

Children's tools can be ordered from TTS Group and other school suppliers. Offer children small saws, and good quality scissors for thinner sheets.

PVA or wood glue is suitable for construction, and you can stick thin sheets of pieces together to make thicker or bigger parts.

## Ideas

Try looking in Yellow Pages for local model making clubs and model makers, who might be willing to give a demonstration.

Investigate Forest Schools and see if you can get involved. There should be a local person to give you advice (try your LA) or look on the Forest Schools site **http://www.forestschools.com/**

## Google Images

Try searching for:

• balsa plane

• balsa model

• wooden plane.

## Books

Some books about wood and carving:

**Models**; Keith Newell; Children's Press

**Leroy's Zoo**: Featuring the Folk Art Carvings of

**Leroy Ramon Archuleta**; Warren Lowe; Black Belt Press

**Daniel's Duck**; Clyde Robert Bulla; HarperTrophy

**Dream Carver**; Diana Cohn; Chronicle Books

**The Christmas Miracle of Jonathan Toomey**; Susan

**Wojciechowski**; Candlewick Press (the story of a woodcarver and a boy)

**The Giant King**; Kathleen Pelley; Child & Family Press - a Scottish story of a woodcarver

**Wood**; Andy Goldsworthy; Harry N. Abrams

# Wax and soap carving

## Previous experience

These materials may be new to children in Key Stage 1, although soap sculpture may have been offered in the Foundation Stage. Children's experiences of candles and soap may have been limited to:

- night lights and other candles in celebrations and birthdays
- perfumed candles for special occasions or in circle times
- writing with candles and paint in wax resist
- using wax crayons
- playing with bars of soap to make bubbles, in play and as part of an activity.

## The responsive adult

In the early stages of working with these materials it is crucial to continue to observe the children. Only by doing this can you set developmentally appropriate challenges and provocations. The ideas listed here are offered as suggestions; the most exciting challenges will arise from children's own interests and motivations, which will only become apparent as you spend time with them, watching and joining them in their play. As you do this, you will be moving between the three interconnecting roles of observer, co-player, extender described below, and will be able to decide what you need to do next to take the learning forward. In three interconnecting roles, the responsive adult will be:

### Observer

- observing
- listening
- interpreting

### Co-player

- modelling
- playing alongside
- offering suggestions
- responding sensitively
- initiating with care!

### Extender

- discussing ideas
- sharing thinking
- modelling new skills
- asking open questions
- being an informed extender
- instigating ideas and thoughts
- supporting children as they make links in learning
- making possibilities evident
- introducing new ideas and resources
- offering challenges and provocations

## Offering challenges and provocations

Soap and wax have similar properties, and can both be carved, using small knives, such as butter knives, or spoons, sharp sticks or pencils. Offer children bargain shop candles, and market stall soap to experiment with, before giving them more complex provocations and challenges.

- Find some candles. Can you:
  - carve them into spirals?
  - carve them into cubes or a cuboids?
  - make name candles, with your own name on?
  - make candle rulers with measurements down the sides?
  - carve them into a sculpture of a pen or pencil?
  - make decorated candles with lines, spots or scratches?
  - stick on objects such as ribbons, leaves, buttons, sequins or beads.

- Use recycled materials to make a celebration holder for night lights or floating candles, and decorate it with found objects.

- Find some bars of soap and soak them in warm water for an hour. What happens? Take a photo of the wet soap.

- What can you do with your soap now? Can you mould it or make it a different shape? See what you can do, and take photos of your creations. What happens to the wet soap creations as they dry?

- Put some birthday candles or wax crayons in a container and put the container somewhere warm (on a radiator, in bright sunshine or in a very low oven). What happens to the wax? Can you change the shape of the crayons or candles now? If you can, make some different shapes that can stand up or hang on a mobile.

- Can you write some secret messages or pictures using white candles to write with. How will your friends know how to see the message?

## Ready for more?

- ◆ Find some bars of soap and use teaspoons, forks or clay tools to carve patterns in the soap. Look on Google Images 'soap carving' for ideas.

- ◆ Collect up as many old wax crayon ends as you can (ask in Reception as well as Years 1 and 2). Now ask an adult to help you to melt the crayons in a jam tart tray. You can sort the crayons into colours or make mixed creations. How can you use your new recycled crayons?

- ◆ Get a grater and grate some crayons or candles. How can you use the grated wax? **http://daycaredaze.wordpress.com/2007/0 2/14/valentine-craft/** will give you one idea. If you grate soap, can you stick it back together again?

- ◆ Look at **http://www.grandandtoy.ca/education/en/pro-melt. asp** and find out how to do melted wax pictures.

- ◆ Can you use some bars of soap to make personalised gifts? You could cut or scratch signs of the zodiac, favourite objects, football badges or illuminated initials by using spoons, nails or screws to make the images. Find the designs you need in Google Images.

- ◆ White soap is really good for making polar bears. Research polar bear images on Google and see if you can make one of your own from a bar of soap. Take photos of the stages of the carving.

## Materials

Try these ideas for free or cheap resources for soap and wax carving:

- ■ bulk buy white kitchen candles;

- ■ offer children tea lights (available in big bags from Ikea) for little or first carving experiences;

- ■ ask parents and colleagues for part-used or unwanted decorative candles;

- ■ buy tablets of bargain soap from supermarkets and market stalls;

- ■ look in sales for decorative candles that may have been slightly damaged.

Tools don't need to be expensive. Collect some of these:

- • old teaspoons
- • blunt knives
- • potato peelers
- • cocktail sticks
- • nails and screws.

## Google Images

- • soap carving
- • wax carving
- • candles
- • decorative candles
- • candle art
- • soap art.

# Materials, websites, books and other references

## Websites

www.associatedcontent.com/article/133198/soap_carving_you_can_do_with_children.html - a 'how to' article.

www.flyingpigs.org.uk/crafts/Soap_Carving.pdf - to download a useful pdf of instructions on soap carving

http://www.workshopnetwork.co.uk/search/details. asp?Artist=355 and artists' workshop with pictures of children making wire, soap and mud sculptures.

www.hitentertainment.com/artattacK/ - the Art Attack site with lots of activities including soap carving, sponge sculptures etc

## Books

Soap Carving: For Children of All Ages; Howard K. Suzuki; Schiffer Publishing

# Shaving foam and spray cream

## Previous experience

Throughout their time in the EYFS, most children will have played with shaving foam as part of messy play. They may have:

- used shaving foam for mark making on
- table tops or in trays
- added different substances to shaving foam, such as lentils, paint, sand, glitter
- manipulated shaving foam underneath cling film or in zip-lock bags
- experimented with making simple temporary sculptures using the foam.

If your children have not played with shaving foam, give them some of these free play experiences before expecting them to concentrate on challenges!

## The responsive adult

In the early stages of working with these materials it is crucial to continue to observe the children. Only by doing this can you set developmentally appropriate challenges and provocations. The ideas listed here are offered as suggestions; the most exciting challenges will arise from children's own interests and motivations, which will only become apparent as you spend time with them, watching and joining them in their play. As you do this, you will be moving between the three interconnecting roles of observer, co-player, extender described below, and will be able to decide what you need to do next to take the learning forward. In three interconnecting roles, the responsive adult will be:

## Observer

- observing
- listening
- interpreting

## Co-player

- modelling
- playing alongside
- offering suggestions
- responding sensitively
- initiating with care!

## Extender

- discussing ideas
- sharing thinking
- modelling new skills
- asking open questions
- being an informed extender
- instigating ideas and thoughts
- supporting children as they make links in learning
- making possibilities evident
- introducing new ideas and resources
- offering challenges and provocations

## Offering challenges and provocations

Make sure you have a camera handy when you offer these resources - sculptures made from foam are shortlived!

- How many different types of sculptures can you make with shaving foam?
- Photograph all your sculptures and use the photographs to make a catalogue of all the sculptures that have been made. Annotate the photographs with comments from their creators!
- Can you make a range of monsters, vehicles or some other theme and photograph your sculptures to make a book? Perhaps some of your creations could form the basis for a story or a poem?
- What is the biggest sculpture that you can make with shaving foam?
- Make lists of important vocabulary or key words in shaving foam. Photograph them for a wall display.
- Try adding powder or ready-mixed paint, glitter and other substances to your foam to create interesting effects.
- Can you create a 'set' or habitat for some small word characters? Try adding leaves, twigs, bark, flowers and other interesting materials?
- Make a range of pretend pies. How many different ways can you decorate them?
- Try doing some mathematical calculations with shaving foam!

- What happens when you leave a foam sculpture for some time, such as a couple of days? Can you take a series of photos or make some drawings to show what happens? Use the photos or drawings to make a flick book, so you can speed up the process.

## Ready for more?

♦ Make some 'combs' from stiff plastic or card (cut some plastic from empty washing-up liquid bottles and flatten it somewhere warm before cutting your combs out). Try the combs out in shaving foam to see what effects you can create. Try forks, kitchen implements and sieves as well.

♦ Hide things in the shaving foam for your friends to find. Once everything has been found, count, classify, and graph the items.

♦ Try marbling with shaving foam. Put about an inch of foam in the bottom of a plastic tray. Use your hand or a piece of card to smooth it out. Now put some water colour paint into a spray bottle and spray colour on to the foam. (Three colours is usually sufficient.) You can then use a paintbrush to pull the colour through the foam. Finally, lay a piece of paper on top of the foam and rub gently to transfer the pattern.

♦ Use the above process, but instead of using water colour use fabric paint. Then you can transfer the design to fabric.

♦ Experiment with whisks in warm water with washing-up liquid. See how many bubbles you can make. Colour the foam with food colouring. Or you could blow the bubbles for foam by using a straw in a mixture of water, food colouring and washing-up liquid or bubble liquid.

# Materials, websites, books and other references

## Materials

Shaving foam is a very inexpensive resource for manipulating and temporary construction. It is easy to use, has very calming effects on some children, and really helps with fine motor skills, as well as creativity.

Spray cream is an alternative for the same activities described here, particularly for children who may be allergic to shaving foam.

Get shaving foam from:

■ bargain chemists or 'pound' shops. Try to get non-allergenic, perfume free varieties.

■ children really don't need tools for this activity, but you could offer spoons, spatulas, scoops and brushes if you wish. Table tops of builders' trays are suitable surfaces for free play. For individual work, offer baking trays, flat plastic containers or lids from ice cream tubs.

■ additions to foam play could include paint, food colouring, aromatherapy oils, glitter or sequins.

■ encourage children to collect and add natural materials such as twigs, flowers or leaves. They may also add small world animals and toys, toy cars or superhero and fantasy figures.

## Ideas

You can make your own foam by whisking soapy water with hand whisks.

## Google Images

Type 'foam city' into Google Images for a great video sequence of a street full of foam.

## Books

**The Little Book of Messy Play**; Sally Featherstone; Featherstone Education

**The Little Book of Mark Making**; Sam Goodman; Featherstone Education

**Children's Arts and Crafts and More Children's Arts and Crafts**; Australian Women's Weekly

**Primary Art and Messy Art**; Mary Ann Kohl; Brilliant Publications

**Adventurous Art**; Susan Milford; Williamson

**Mudworks**; Mary Ann Kohl; Bright Ring

# Fruit and vegetables

## Previous experience

During their time in the Foundation Stage most children will have worked with fruit and vegetables in a variety of ways. They may have:

- printed with potatoes and other vegetables, drawn these objects and made close observations of their features

- made soups and stews, cutting up and looking at vegetables

- prepared a variety of fruit and vegetables for snack time, including fruit kebabs, fruit jellies, individual pizzas

- played with fruit and vegetables as part of home corner play

- been involved in visiting the greengrocers to buy fruit and vegetables, or grown their own.

## The responsive adult

In the early stages of working with these materials it is crucial to continue to observe the children. Only by doing this can you set developmentally appropriate challenges and provocations. The ideas listed here are offered as suggestions; the most exciting challenges will arise from children's own interests and motivations, which will only become apparent as you spend time with them, watching and joining them in their play. As you do this, you will be moving between the three interconnecting roles of observer, co-player, extender described below, and will be able to decide what you need to do next to take the learning forward. In three interconnecting roles, the responsive adult will be:

### Observer

- observing
- listening
- interpreting

### Co-player

- modelling
- playing alongside
- offering suggestions
- responding sensitively
- initiating with care!

### Extender

- discussing ideas
- sharing thinking
- modelling new skills
- asking open questions
- being an informed extender
- instigating ideas and thoughts
- supporting children as they make links in learning
- making possibilities evident
- introducing new ideas and resources
- offering challenges and provocations

## Offering challenges and provocations

Experience of looking at and using fruit and vegetables decoratively in cooking and other food preparation will give children a knowledge to build on as they take on more complex challenges.

- If you don't already have it get a copy of *How Are You Peeling? Foods with Moods* by Saxton Freyman and Joost Elffers (Arthur A. Levine Books/Scholastic). This is an excellent book that can be used as a real source of inspiration. The authors have made use of a wide variety of fruit and vegetables and sculpted with them to depict a range of emotions. Once the children have explored the book they will be really keen to have a go for themselves. Or you could Google 'sculpting with fruit and vegetables' and look at other examples.

- Can you use fruit and vegetable to make characters that are, for example, angry, disappointed, excited, nervous, sad? Can you photograph your characters to make your own book of Foods with Moods?

- Can you make some fruit and vegetable characters and write a story for them? Can you illustrate your story with photographs of your characters? You could make the Potato Family, Carrot Family, Parsnip Family, etc.

- Can you squeeze some juices to make smoothies from your fruit and vegetables? Try different flavours and combinations and hold a survey to find which are most popular. Graph the results. Set up a smoothie bar and write a menu of all the different drinks available. Invite other children or parents to a smoothie party.

- Make your own recipe book of smoothies you have designed.

- Can you make some fruit kebabs? Experiment with fruits, colours and patterns to make new combinations.

## Ready for more?

♦ Choose a traditional tale, for example *The Three Little Pigs*. Can you make the characters out of fruit and vegetables?

♦ Can you create fillings for stuffing tomatoes, mushrooms, peppers and apples? Try them out on your friends. Which are the most popular?

♦ Google 'Pumpkin Lanterns'. Can you create some pumpkin lanterns

♦ Can you make lanterns from any other fruit and vegetables?

♦ Can you create fillings for lettuce and cabbage leaves, or vine leaves?

♦ Can you create your own recipe book for stuffed fruit and vegetables? Use photographs of your own creations as a basis for the book. Get your friends to write reviews of your creations.

♦ Can you make a sorbet with an orange or a lemon and serve it in the original skin?

♦ Can you make a pomander using oranges or lemons? How many different ways can you find to decorate it?

♦ Get some dried peas and soak them overnight in water. Now use the peas and some cocktail sticks to make some sculptures. You could try adding chickpeas or other dried beans or seeds. What sorts of sculptures can you make? Can you make these objects into a ball structure, or a tower?

## Materials

Fruit and vegetables are cheap resources for art work and construction. Ask local greengrocers or market traders for any bargains they may have, and remember that potatoes, turnips, carrots and swede are cheap basic ingredients.

For some more unusual creations try:

■ packets of vine leaves

■ peppers and aubergines

■ pot pourri

■ dried peas or tinned chick peas with cocktail sticks

■ add 'googly eyes', beads, sequins, mapping pins, wire.

## Ideas

Collect some baskets or boxes of stones, leaves, nuts, feathers, cones and other natural objects — replenish these by removing the old ones and replacing with collections from recent walks, visits, holidays and so on. Always encourage children to pick up natural materials for the collection, and ask them to bring in a shell, pebble, cone, leaf or a piece of driftwood from their holidays and you'll soon have a collection! The message about collecting natural objects should always be 'If it isn't fixed on, it is likely to be OK. If it is fixed on - ask!' Buy pot pourri, polished pebbles, glass beads from bargain shops. Ask local florists or market traders for 'past their sell by' flowers to use for Rangoli and other art works.

## Google Images

- natural art
- art from nature
- Andy Goldsworthy
- natural collage
- pebble art
- painted stone
- rangoli
- petals
- leaves.

# Materials, websites, books and other references

## Websites

Look up **Rangoli** on the internet and find out about this form of art, originally found on doorsteps. You can also download versions of rangoli patterns to use as bases for your creations with real petals, leaves, sand etc. Try www.activityvillage. co.uk/rangoli.htm or http://www.ehow.com/

This site has pattern templates to download — http://www.dltkkids. com/World/india/mrangoli.htm

## Books

**Nature Crafts for Kids**; Gwen Diehn; Sterling Juvenile;

**Arts in the School Grounds**; Brian Keaney; Learning Through Landscapes

**Hands-on Nature**; Jenepher Lingelbach; University Press of New England

**Nature's Playground**; Fiona Danks; Frances Lincoln

**Ecoart!**; Lauri Carlson; Williamson Publishing

# Stuffing

## Previous experience

While in the EYFS most children will have spent time stuffing things inside other things as part of schematic play. All early years practitioners will be familiar with the child who takes a bag into the home corner and stuffs it full with the resources that the other children are trying to play with! Children may also have:

- stuffed paper bags or socks to make simple puppets
- stuffed old clothes to make Guy Fawkes or other figures
- stuffed various containers with newspaper and other materials as part of their free play in the workshop area.

## The responsive adult

In the early stages of working with these materials it is crucial to continue to observe the children. Only by doing this can you set developmentally appropriate challenges and provocations. The ideas listed here are offered as suggestions; the most exciting challenges will arise from children's own interests and motivations, which will only become apparent as you spend time with them, watching and joining them in their play. As you do this, you will be moving between the three interconnecting roles of observer, co-player, extender described below, and will be able to decide what you need to do next to take the learning forward. In three interconnecting roles, the responsive adult will be:

### Observer

- observing
- listening
- interpreting

### Co-player

- modelling
- playing alongside
- offering suggestions
- responding sensitively
- initiating with care!

### Extender

- discussing ideas
- sharing thinking
- modelling new skills
- asking open questions
- being an informed extender
- instigating ideas and thoughts
- supporting children as they make links in learning
- making possibilities evident
- introducing new ideas and resources
- offering challenges and provocations

## Offering challenges and provocations

Enclosing something inside something else is a concept that pre-occupies many pre-school children and it is usually possible to find a few children in Year 1 for whom enclosing is still important:

- How many different materials can you identify that would be suitable for stuffing things? Work with your friends to make a list, then collect some of the materials and experiment.

- Can you design or think of some characters that could be made by stuffing old clothes?

- How many different ways can you find to make the hands/body/face for a stuffed character?

- Once you have made your characters, can you write an adventure story for them? Perhaps you could take photographs to illustrate your story and make a Power Point presentation.

- How many different things can you make by stuffing old tights, for example, could you make a beanstalk for a role play of Jack and the Beanstalk, or a sea serpent for a pirate story?

- What is the longest creature you can make? Can you find out how long the Loch Ness Monster is thought to be?

- Can you make some scary monsters by stuffing old tights? Use string, wire, buttons, sequins and metal objects to help make your creations more interesting!

- Can you make some puppet characters from old socks? How many different types of creatures can you make? Why not make a puppet theatre by hanging a piece of fabric from hooks halfway up the frame of a door. Now write a play for your characters and invite some other children to watch.

- Can you make your own stuffed toy? It can be any sort, even a creature that has never existed.

## Ready for more?

- Design and make some doorstops or draught stoppers. What will you put inside them to make them heavy enough to hold a door open or keep out a real draught? Google 'fabric doorstop' or 'draught stopper' for some ideas.

- Can you make a collection of unwanted soft toys and turn them into doorstops by undoing a seam and placing something heavy inside?

- Can you make your own bean bags and invent some games to play with them?

- Make your own cushion or pillow.

- Can you make some 'smelly bags' by stuffing material with flowers or herbs?

- Design and make a bed for a pet.

- Instead of putting stuffing into something, why not try taking the stuffing OUT of some old stuffed toys so that you can turn them into puppets! Make sure you ask first!

- Try stuffing some vegetables. Which vegetables are best for stuffing and what ingredients would be good? Can you find some recipes or make up some of your own? See if you can get hold of a marrow and invent some recipes for stuffed marrow. Try your stuffed vegetables out on your friends and make a graph to show which recipes are the most popular!

# Materials, websites, books and other references

## Materials

If you want to buy new wadding, try:
www.hobbycraft.co.uk/ideas_library/idea_87.html — for filling for toys and a reindeer draught stopper.

Other materials for stuffing toys and simple items are plentiful and cheap. Try:

- sheep's wool collected from hedges and fences
- torn-up fabric
- paper shreddings
- polystyrene beads or 'wiggles'
- newspaper
- hay or straw
- cotton wool
- cotton wadding.

## Google images

Suggestions for words to search:

- stuffed toys
- stuffed animals
- soft toys

## Websites

There are lots of ideas on the Internet for simple stuffing activities to make toys and other items. Try:

http://rubyglen.com/crafts/snowman.htm
for a simple snowman doorstop

http://www.thriftyfun.com/tf957998.tip.html
for draught stoppers made from socks

http://jas.familyfun.go.com/arts-and-crafts?page=CraftDisplay&craftid=11565
for draught stoppers

http://www.allcrafts.net/dolls.htm#freeprojects
for free doll-making instructions.

## Books

**Dogger**; Shirley Hughes; Red Fox

**Stupid Sock Creatures**; Making Quirky, Lovable Figures from Cast-off Socks; John Murphy; Lark Books

**Bean Bag Toys**; Kathryn Severns; KP Books

**Easy-to-Make Stuffed Dinosaurs**; Zillah Halls; Dover

**Make Your Own Teddy Bears and Bear Clothes (Quick Starts for Kids!)**; Jodie Davis; Williamson

**Make Your Own Toys (Recycling Fun)**; Five Mile Press

# Moulding

## Previous experience

Children may have already had experience of moulding with play resources in the following ways:

- using sand moulds for mud, sand, or compost
- using moulds for jellies and other foods
- moulding clay or dough
- moulding other malleable materials such as paper pulp
- looking at footprints and other marks in mud, sand etc.

## The responsive adult

In the early stages of working with these materials it is crucial to continue to observe the children. Only by doing this can you set developmentally appropriate challenges and provocations. The ideas listed here are offered as suggestions; the most exciting challenges will arise from children's own interests and motivations, which will only become apparent as you spend time with them, watching and joining them in their play. As you do this, you will be moving between the three interconnecting roles of observer, co-player, extender described below, and will be able to decide what you need to do next to take the learning forward. In three interconnecting roles, the responsive adult will be:

### Observer

- observing
- listening
- interpreting

### Co-player

- modelling
- playing alongside
- offering suggestions
- responding sensitively
- initiating with care!

### Extender

- discussing ideas
- sharing thinking
- modelling new skills
- asking open questions
- being an informed extender
- instigating ideas and thoughts
- supporting children as they make links in learning
- making possibilities evident
- introducing new ideas and resources
- offering challenges and provocations

## Offering challenges and provocations

Children will almost certainly have used manufactured moulds for sand and dough. They may never have thought about how to make moulds from familiar objects, or using one object to make a mould for multiple objects. Give older children plenty of time to experience and discuss activities which build on their earlier knowledge.

- Use some sand or dough moulds to make shapes in sand, dough or mud. How do moulds work?

- Can you make a mould from recycled materials? You could try some of these:

  - the insides from chocolate or sweet boxes;
  - cups of all sorts, including paper and plastic cups;
  - foil cases from jam tarts and pies;
  - aerosol, bottle and tin lids;
  - buckets, plastic boxes, egg cartons.

  Try your moulds with sand, dough or mud, or fill them with water and freeze them.

- Tear some strips of newspaper and try pasting them over a mould such as:

  - a balloon;
  - a plastic bowl;
  - a plastic toy such as a big dinosaur figure;
  - a wellington boot;
  - a cardboard box.

  Keep pasting layers until the structure is firm, and leave to dry. Now work out a way to get the paper shape off the mould. You may have to cut it. Look inside the paper mould, what can you see?

- Use jelly moulds to make jellies, blancmange or ice sculptures from coloured water.

- Get some shallow tin lids and bowls, and make bird food sculptures by filling the lids with bird seed, adding water and freezing overnight. Tip the ice sculptures out, leave them outside and watch the birds come to eat the seeds.

## Ready for more?

◆ If you enjoyed making bird food moulds, try making some bird cake. Look at **http://www.rspb.org.uk/youth/makeanddo/ activities/ birdcake.asp** to find out how to make bird cakes to hang outside in winter.

◆ Find some small, clean things to use as moulds - you could use small cups or very clean yogurt pots. Fill these with cooked rice and make a healthy snack salad with shredded lettuce and rice castles, decorated with pieces of tomato, cucumber and cooked peas.

◆ Can you make a mould of a plastic animal, so you can make lots of copies? You need to choose a small model with a chunky body and short legs. Now try making a mould from sand or plaster. Once you have your mould, you will be able to make more copies of the animal.

◆ Make some healthy ice lollies. Use fruit juices and small pieces of fruit to fill ice lolly moulds. Freeze them and share them with you friends.

◆ Or make some savoury ice lollies from tomato juice, with peas, beans and small pieces of vegetable. Try these and see who likes them!

◆ Can you make a striped jelly or a rainbow jelly? Or can you make a jelly with real fruit pieces in it? Look at **www.nigella. com/recipes** for instructions, or 'rainbow jelly' in Google Images.

## Materials

Moulds can be made from lots of different items — it only needs a good imagination and lots of recycled containers:

- liners from chocolate and sweet boxes
- bowls, mugs, cups and pots
- jelly moulds from junk shops and rummage sales
- plastic and polystyrene cups
- boxes, packets, tins
- plant pots and containers.

Use some of the following for moulding:

- cooked rice
- damp sand
- clay or mud
- dough or pastry
- jelly
- plaster or DIY filler
- aspic jelly (good for savoury moulds with vegetables set in them).

## Google images

- jelly mould
- jelly baby
- sandcastle
- blancmange
- giant jelly

# Materials, websites, books and other references

## Websites

Google web search for information on suppliers of jelly moulds and party food making:

http://www.jellyandblancmange.co.uk — has children's cooking equipment.

## Books

Don't Put Your Finger in the Jelly Nelly; Nick Sharratt; Scholastic

Developing Science in the Primary Classroom; Wynne Harlen; Longman

The Little Book of Science Through Art; Sally Featherstone; Featherstone Education

Guzzling Jelly with Giant Gorbelly; John Rice; Macmillan

Party Food; Sharon Dalgleish; Smart Apple Media

# Fabric

## Previous experience

There will be very few children who will not, at some time in the EYFS, have used fabrics for different sorts of activities such as:

- fabric for collage
- making dens and shelters
- with clips and pegs for dressing up
- for wrapping and covering
- for painting or spraying colour on
- for hangings, decorations etc.

The challenge for Key Stage 1 teachers is to:

- support children in expanding the challenge and complexity of their use of fabrics
- help children understand how fabrics are designed and made, and how colour and patterns are added.

## The responsive adult

In the early stages of working with these materials it is crucial to continue to observe the children. Only by doing this can you set developmentally appropriate challenges and provocations. The ideas listed here are offered as suggestions; the most exciting challenges will arise from children's own interests and motivations, which will only become apparent as you spend time with them, watching and joining them in their play. As you do this, you will be moving between the three interconnecting roles of observer, co-player, extender described below, and will be able to decide what you need to do next to take the learning forward. In three interconnecting roles, the responsive adult will be:

### Observer

- observing
- listening
- interpreting

### Co-player

- modelling
- playing alongside
- offering suggestions
- responding sensitively
- initiating with care!

### Extender

- discussing ideas
- sharing thinking
- modelling new skills
- asking open questions
- being an informed extender
- instigating ideas and thoughts
- supporting children as they make links in learning
- making possibilities evident
- introducing new ideas and resources
- offering challenges and provocations

## Offering challenges and provocations

Collect samples of as many fabrics as you can find. Make sure you keep some to experiment with and explore in scientific activities as well as plenty of fabric for free choice in creative and design work.

- How many different sorts of fabric can your find in your school? Take a camera with you and photograph all the different sorts.
- Can you make a fabric sample book with photos and samples of different fabrics and what they are used for?
- Find some fabrics and design and make a patchwork quilt picture. Look on the Internet for some ideas. You could sew the pieces or stick them on paper or card.
- Can you design and make one of the following:
  - a hammock for an action doll or superhero figure;
  - a cloak for a magician;
  - a flag for football or another sport;
  - a line of triangular flags of different colours.

- Find a magnifying glass and look very closely at some different sorts of fabric. What can you see? If you have a camera with a zoom, take some close-up photos of the fabrics you have chosen. Use the photos and the fabrics to make a display quiz where your friend must match the photos with the correct fabrics.
- Collect some fabric samples and try to take them apart to find out how they have been made. Draw what you find and make your drawings into a book about fabrics.
- Make a hanging with a long strip of lightweight fabric and some natural materials such as leaves, twigs, seeds and grass. Hang your creation up from a cane or piece of dowelling in your classroom or a corridor. Could you make a weatherproof version for outside?

## Ready for more?

- Make a weaving loom on your classroom door. There are instructions on **http://www.associatedcontent.com/article/ 257924/easy_weaving_for_kids_make_textile.html?cat=24** .You will need to collect some ribbon and wool.

- Now, can you make your own loom from a strong box or an old picture frame? Collect all the things you need before you start.

- Can you work with some friends to find a way of making fabric waterproof? Set up an experiment to find out and test the best way to do this.

- Collect some fabric scraps and make some clothes for superhero figures, dolls or soft toys. You could turn them into other characters, or dress them for new adventures.

- Now make a bed and a room for your character and decorate it with fabrics, curtains, sheets and pillows.

- Design some new fabrics. Do these first on paper, and look for ideas in books or on Google Images 'fabric designs'. When you have designed your fabric, can you transfer it to real fabric, using fabric crayons, pens or paint?

- Find a way to test the stretchiness of some fabrics. You will need a friend to work with, a camera and some way of recording what you find out. What makes fabric stretchy? Can you use the Internet to find out about Lycra and elastic?

## Materials

Fabric is a cheap and endlessly versatile resource. If you get a bargain length, trade with a colleague so you both get a range of sorts and textures. Try:

- asking parents and colleagues for unwanted (but clean) clothing, curtains, furnishing fabrics

- collecting plastic, vinyl, fur and wool fabrics for added interest and experiment

- looking in charity shops for fabrics

- asking for samples of carpets, curtains, ends of rolls and other fabrics from furnishing stores

- looking in haberdashery departments for remnants

- trying fabric stalls on markets, where you might get roll ends.

## Google Images

- fabric
- fabric design
- patterned fabric
- sari fabric
- woollen fabric

- silk fabric
- sari fabric
- fabric wrapping
- wrapped art.

Try putting '**Christo**' in Google, or Google Images to find out about an amazing artist who wraps whole buildings and landscapes in fabric. He has wrapped buildings in Germany, a whole canyon, some islands and even the trees in Central Park in New York!

# Materials, websites, books and other references

## Websites

Google **fabric artists** will give you links to some really interesting artists who work in fabrics and collage, and 'fabric art display primary school' will link to some schools. Try the galleries at
**http://www.kidsatart.org/showcase4.php** or **http://www.durhamlea.org.uk/galleries**
and there are hundreds of others!
**http://www.creative-partnerships.com/projects** is the home of Creative Partnerships, an Arts Council project that supports artists working with children of all ages in schools across the country.

## Books

**Angela Weaves a Dream: The Story of a Young Maya Artist**; Michele Sola; Disney Press

**Threads, Yarn and Fabric Projects**; Marcia Riley; Stackpole Books

**Sewing with Felt**; Buff McAllister; Boyds Mills

**Easy to Make Felt Bean Bag Toys**; Jane Erthe; Dover Publications

**My First Sewing Book**; Cherry Palmer-Pletsch Associates

# Combined materials

## Previous experience

Children's experience of combining materials will very much depend on the philosophy of the setting they have attended. If they have been to a setting which encouraged them to access materials freely they may well have had extensive opportunities to combine materials in a wide variety of different ways, such as:

- in free play indoors and outside
- in free play in the workshop area
- to test and explore the properties of different materials
- when making props for role play
- in home corner play
- to represent objects and experiences in their own lives.

## The responsive adult

In the early stages of working with these materials it is crucial to continue to observe the children. Only by doing this can you set developmentally appropriate challenges and provocations. The ideas listed here are offered as suggestions; the most exciting challenges will arise from children's own interests and motivations, which will only become apparent as you spend time with them, watching and joining them in their play. As you do this, you will be moving between the three interconnecting roles of observer, co-player, extender described below, and will be able to decide what you need to do next to take the learning forward. In three interconnecting roles, the responsive adult will be:

### Observer

- observing
- listening
- interpreting

### Co-player

- modelling
- playing alongside
- offering suggestions
- responding sensitively
- initiating with care!

### Extender

- discussing ideas
- sharing thinking
- modelling new skills
- asking open questions
- being an informed extender
- instigating ideas and thoughts
- supporting children as they make links in learning
- making possibilities evident
- introducing new ideas and resources
- offering challenges and provocations

## Offering challenges and provocations

In order to get the most out of games, children first need to build up a wide repertoire of the properties and uses of different materials. Once they have done this, they can innovate and make up new versions, using their creativity to invent and expand on their knowledge.

- Can you use a combination of materials to make a character, vehicle or other type of sculpture?

- Can you make a character or structure using two, three or four different types of materials, for example, clay, wire and wood?

- Can you combine materials to make a 'set' for a story book, for example, *We're Going on a Bear Hunt*. How will you make the snow/forest/swishy grass etc.?

- Can you make a structure or sculpture using:
  - wire and clay?
  - soap and wire?
  - foam and wood?
  - other materials from your classroom?

- When you combine clay and wire, how many different ways can you find of using the wire?

- Can you make a piece of jewellery from a combination of materials?

- Look at all the pages in this book. Can you make a sculpture, an environment for a story, a vehicle or an abacus using the materials listed in this book?

- Look at the recycled resources that you have collected in your school or your class. How can you combine some of these resources with the ideas in this book to make an outdoor sculpture. Work with your friends and see if you can make:
  - a sculpture with moving parts;
  - a sculpture that makes people laugh;
  - a sculpture of a group of animals.

## Ready for more?

- Can you write some ideas books about different ways to use the materials in this book, for example, Ten Exciting Things to Make With Soap?

- Can you use a combination of materials to make dream catchers, mobiles, Christmas or Divali decorations?

- Can you work in a group or class to make a sculpture for the wall in your hall, using a combination of the materials in this book?

- Can you find out who likes which materials best and represent the results of your survey on a graph? Ask the children to tell you which materials they like using and which materials they like looking at.

- Can you make a wall hanging for your reading area or library with a combination of materials? Work in groups to try different combinations. Which works the best? Which is easiest to display?

- Can you make some lanterns using a combination of materials? Which materials would be best? How could you make your lanterns light up?

- Can you design a set of characters for a story and make them using a combination of materials? Can you turn your story into a Power Point display or a video to show to other classes?

# Materials, websites, books and other references

## Materials

This section is where recycled materials can really come into their own. Locate your local Children's Scrapstore by looking on www.childrensscrapstore.co.uk and using the Directory. If you have never used this service it is a great find!

You can also recycle your own materials and get the children involved too. Make sure they always wash the items before they bring them to school, and get parents' permission to collect things. You could start with:

- plastic containers of all sorts
- planks, tyres, fabrics and cable reels
- boxes, bags and baskets
- wire, bag ties, bubble wrap, card and paper
- old clothes, scarves, hats etc for stuffing
- foil containers, boxes etc.

It's important to give children plenty of time to work on their projects, providing a camera for them to record their own progress for discussions and evaluation.

## Google Images

To look at some recycled art and sculpture, try

- recycled art
- african recycled art.

## Websites

Google: There are lots of sites related to recycling, for information and details of local projects.

http://www.ecofriend.org - has a great recycled dinosaur

http://www.inhabitat.com has some cars and motor bikes.

## Books

EarthFriendly Toys: Make Toys and Games from Reusable Objects (Earth-Friendly); George Pfiffner; Jossey Bass

Cups and Cans and Paper Plates; Craft Projects from Recycled Materials; Phyllis Fiarotta; Sterling

Make Sculptures! ; Kim Solga; North Light Books

Kids Create: Art and Craft Experience for 3 to 9 Year Olds; Lauri Carlson; Williamson Publishing

Art and Crafts for Kids; Australian Women's Weekly; Susan Tomnay; ACP

Children's Art and Crafts; Australian Women's Weekly; Maryanne Blacker; ACP

| **Literacy 1**<br>Speaking | • Retell stories, ordering events using story language<br>• Tell stories and describe incidents from their own experience in an audible voice.<br>• Interpret a text by reading aloud with some variety in pace and emphasis<br>• Experiment with and build new stores of words to communicate in different contexts. | **Literacy 6**<br>Word structure and spelling | • Spell new words using phonics as the prime approach<br>• Segment sounds into their constituent phonemes in order to spell them correctly. Children move from spelling simple CVC words to longer words that include common diagraphs & adjacent consonants such as 'brush', 'crunch'<br>• Recognise and use alternative ways of spelling the graphemes already taught, for example that the /ae/ sound can be spelt with 'ai', 'ay' or 'a-e'; that the /ee/ sound can also be spelt as 'ea' and 'e'; & begin to know which words contain which spelling alternatives<br>• Use knowledge of common inflections in spelling, such as plurals, -ly, -er<br>• Read and spell phonically decodable two and three syllable words. | **Literacy 8**<br>Engaging and responding to text | • Select books for personal reading and give reasons for choices<br>• Visualise and comment on events, characters and ideas, making imaginative links to their own experiences<br>• Distinguish fiction and nonfiction texts and the different purposes for reading them. |
| **Literacy 2**<br>Listening and responding | • Listen with sustained concentration, building new stores of words in different contexts<br>• Listen to tapes or video and express views about how a story or information has been presented<br>• Listen to and follow instructions accurately, asking for help and clarification if necessary. | | | **Literacy 9**<br>Creating and shaping texts | • Independently choose what to write about, plan and follow it through<br>• Use key features of narrative in their own writing<br>• Convey information and ideas in simple non-narrative forms<br>• Find and use new and interesting words and phrases, including story language<br>• Create short simple texts on paper and on screen that combine words with images (and sounds). |
| **Literacy 3**<br>Group discussion & interaction | • Take turns to speak, listen to others' suggestions and talk about what they are going to do<br>• Ask and answer questions, make relevant contributions, offer suggestions and take turns<br>• Explain their views to others in a small group, decide how to report the group's views to the class. | **Literacy 7**<br>Understanding and interpreting texts | • Identify the main events and characters in stories, and find specific information in simple texts<br>• Use syntax and context when reading for meaning<br>• Make predictions showing an understanding of ideas, events and characters<br>• Recognise the main elements that shape different texts<br>• Explore the effect of patterns of language and repeated words and phrases. | **Literacy 10**<br>Text structure and organisation | • Write chronological and non-chronological texts using simple structures<br>• Group written sentences together in chunks of meaning or subject. |
| **Literacy 4**<br>Drama | • Explore familiar themes and characters through improvisation and role-play<br>• Act out their own and well-known stories, using voices for characters<br>• Discuss why they like a performance. | | | **Literacy 11**<br>Sentence structure and punctuation | • Compose and write simple sentences independently to communicate meaning<br>• Use capital letters and full stops when punctuating simple sentences. |
| **Literacy 5**<br>Word recognition, coding and decoding | • Recognise and use alternative ways of pronouncing the graphemes already taught, for example, that the grapheme 'g' is pronounced differently in 'get' and 'gem'; the grapheme 'ow' is pronounced differently in 'how' and 'show'<br>• Recognise and use alternative ways of spelling the phonemes already taught, for example 'ae'' can be spelt with 'ai', 'ay' or 'a-e'; begin to know which words contain which spelling alternatives.<br>• Identify the constituent parts of two-syllable and three-syllable words to support the application of phonic knowledge and skills. Recognise automatically an increasing number of familiar high frequency words | • Apply phonic knowledge and skills as the prime approach to reading and spelling unfamiliar words that are not completely decodable<br>• Read more challenging texts which can be decoded using their acquired phonic knowledge and skills; automatic recognition of high frequency words. Read and spell phonically decodable two-syllable and three-syllable words. | **Literacy 12**<br>Presentation | • Write most letters, correctly formed and orientated, using a comfortable and efficient pencil grip<br>• Write with spaces between words accurately<br>• Use the space bar and keyboard to type their name and simple texts. |

| **Literacy 1**<br>Speaking | • Speak with clarity and use appropriate intonation when reading and reciting texts<br>• Tell real and imagined stories using the conventions of familiar story language<br>• Explain ideas and processes using imaginative and adventurous vocabulary and nonverbal gestures to support communication |
|---|---|
| **Literacy 2**<br>Listening and responding | • Listen to others in class, ask relevant questions and follow instructions<br>• Listen to talk by an adult, remember some specific points and identify what they have learned<br>• Respond to presentations by describing characters, repeating some highlight and commenting constructively |
| **Literacy 3**<br>Group discussion and interaction | • Ensure that everyone contributes, allocate tasks, and consider alternatives and reach agreement<br>• Work effectively in groups by ensuring that each group member takes a turn challenging, supporting and moving on<br>• Listen to each other's views and preferences, agree the next steps to take and identify contributions by each group member |
| **Literacy 4**<br>Drama | • Adopt appropriate roles in small or large groups and consider alternative courses of action<br>• Present part of traditional stories, their own stories or work drawn from different parts of the curriculum for members of their own class<br>• Consider how mood and atmosphere are created in live or recorded performance |

| **Literacy 5**<br>Word recognition, coding and decoding | • Read independently and with increasing fluency longer and less familiar texts<br>• Spell with increasing accuracy and confidence, drawing on word recognition and knowledge of word structure, and spelling patterns<br>• Know how to tackle unfamiliar words that are not completely decodable<br>• Read and spell less common alternative graphemes including trigraphs<br>• Read high and medium frequency words independently and automatically |
|---|---|
| **Literacy 6**<br>Word structure and spelling | • Spell with increasing accuracy and confidence, drawing on word recognition and knowledge of word structure, and spelling patterns including common inflections and use of double letters<br>• Read and spell less common alternative graphemes including trigraphs |
| **Literacy 7**<br>Understanding and interpreting texts | • Draw together ideas and information from across a whole text, using simple signposts in the text<br>• Give reasons why things happen or characters change<br>• Explain organisational features of texts, including alphabetical order, layout, diagrams etc<br>• Use syntax and context to build their store of vocabulary when reading<br>• Explore how particular words are used, including words and expressions with similar meanings |
| **Literacy 8**<br>Engaging and responding to text | • Read whole books on their own, choosing and justifying selections<br>• Engage with books through exploring and enacting interpretations<br>• Explain their reactions to texts, commenting on important aspects |

| **Literacy 9**<br>Creating and shaping texts | • Draw on knowledge and experience of texts in deciding and planning what and how to write<br>• Sustain form in narrative, including use of person and time<br>• Maintain consistency in non-narrative, including purpose and tense<br>• Make adventurous word and language choices appropriate to the style and purpose of the text<br>• Select from different presentational features to suit particular writing purposes on paper and on screen |
|---|---|
| **Literacy 10**<br>Text structure and organisation | • Use planning to establish clear sections for writing<br>• Use appropriate language to make sections hang together |
| **Literacy 11**<br>Sentence structure and punctuation | • Write simple and compound sentences and begin to use subordination in relation to time and reason<br>• Compose sentences using tense consistently (present and past)<br>• Use question marks, and use commas to separate items in a list |
| **Literacy 12**<br>Presentation | • Write legibly, using upper and lower case letters appropriately within words, and observing correct spacing within and between words<br>• Form and use the four basic handwriting joins<br>• Word process short narrative and non-narrative texts |

| | | | |
|---|---|---|---|
| **Mathematics 1**<br><br>Using and applying maths | • Solve problems involving counting, adding, subtracting, doubling or halving in the context of numbers, measures or money, for example to 'pay' and 'give change'<br><br>• Describe a puzzle or problem using numbers, practical materials and diagrams; use these to solve the problem and set the solution in the original context<br><br>• Answer a question by selecting and using suitable equipment, and sorting information, shapes or objects; display results using tables and pictures<br><br>• Describe simple patterns and relationships involving numbers or shapes; decide whether examples satisfy given conditions<br><br>• Describe ways of solving puzzles and problems, explaining choices and decisions orally or using pictures | **Mathematics 4**<br><br>Calculating | • Relate addition to counting on; recognise that addition can be done in any order; use practical and informal written methods to support the addition of a one-digit number or a multiple of 10 to a one-digit or two-digit number<br><br>• Understand subtraction as 'take away' and find a 'difference' by counting up; use practical and informal written methods to support the subtraction of a one-digit number from a one-digit or two digit number and a multiple of 10 from a two-digit number<br><br>• Solve practical problems that involve combining groups of 2, 5 or 10, or sharing into equal groups<br><br>• Use the vocabulary related to addition and subtraction and symbols to describe and record addition and subtraction number sentences |
| **Mathematics 2**<br><br>Counting and understanding numbers | • Count reliably at least 20 objects, recognising that when rearranged the number of objects stays the same; estimate a number of objects that can be checked by counting<br><br>• Compare and order numbers, using the related vocabulary; use the equals (=) sign<br><br>• Read and write numerals from 0 to 20, then beyond; use knowledge of place value to position these numbers on a number track and number line<br><br>• Say the number that is 1 more or less than any given number, and 10 more or less for multiples of 10<br><br>• Use the vocabulary of halves and quarters in context | **Mathematics 5**<br><br>Understanding shape | • Visualise and name common 2-D shapes and 3-D solids and describe their features; use them to make patterns, pictures and models<br><br>• Identify objects that turn about a point (e.g. scissors) or about a line (e.g. a door); recognise and make whole, half and quarter turns<br><br>• Visualise and use everyday language to describe the position of objects and direction and distance when moving them, for example when placing or moving objects on a game board |
| | | **Mathematics 6**<br><br>Measuring | • Estimate, measure, weigh and compare objects, choosing and using suitable uniform non-standard or standard units and measuring instruments (e.g. a lever balance, metre stick or measuring jug)<br><br>• Use vocabulary related to time; order days of the week and months; read the time to the hour and half hour |
| **Mathematics 3**<br><br>Knowing and using number facts | • Derive and recall all pairs of numbers with a total of 10 and addition facts for totals to at least 5; work out the corresponding subtraction facts<br><br>• Count on or back in ones, twos, fives and tens and use this knowledge to derive the multiples of 2, 5 and 10 to the tenth multiple<br><br>• Recall the doubles of all numbers to at least 10 | **Mathematics 7**<br><br>Handling data | • Answer a question by recording information in lists and tables; present outcomes using practical resources, pictures, block graphs or pictograms<br><br>• Use diagrams to sort objects into groups according to a given criterion; suggest a different criterion for grouping the same objects |

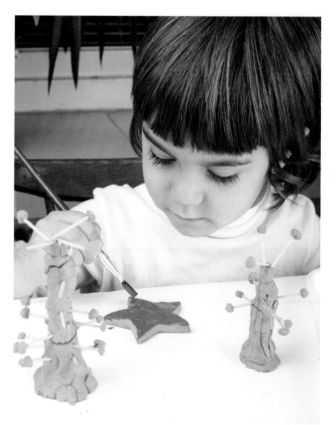

## Mathematics 1

Using and applying maths

- Solve problems involving addition, subtraction, multiplication or division in contexts of numbers, measures or pounds and pence
- Identify and record the information or calculation needed to solve a puzzle or problem; carry out the steps or calculations and check the solution in the context of the problem
- Follow a line of enquiry; answer questions by choosing and using suitable equipment and selecting, organising and presenting information in lists, tables and simple diagrams
- Describe patterns and relationships involving numbers or shapes, make predictions and test these with examples
- Present solutions to puzzles and problems in an organised way; explain decisions, methods and results in pictorial, spoken or written form, using mathematical language and number sentences

## Mathematics 2

Counting and understanding numbers

- Read and write two-digit and three-digit numbers in figures and words; describe and extend number sequences and recognise odd and even numbers
- Count up to 100 objects by grouping them and counting in tens, fives or twos; explain what each digit in a two-digit number represents, including numbers where 0 is a place holder; partition two-digit numbers in different ways, including into multiples of 10 and 1
- Order two-digit numbers and position them on a number line; use the greater than (>) and less than (<) signs
- Estimate a number of objects; round two-digit numbers to the nearest 10
- Find one half, one quarter and three quarters of shapes and sets of objects

## Mathematics 3

Knowing and using number facts

- Derive and recall all addition and subtraction facts for each number to at least 10, all pairs with totals to 20 and all pairs of multiples of 10 with totals up to 100
- Understand that halving is the inverse of doubling and derive and recall doubles of all numbers to 20, and the corresponding halves
- Derive and recall multiplication facts for the 2, 5 and 10 times-tables and the related division facts; recognise multiples of 2, 5 and 10
- Use knowledge of number facts and operations to estimate and check answers to calculations

## Mathematics 4

Calculating

- Add or subtract mentally a one-digit number or a multiple of 10 to or from any two-digit number; use practical and informal written methods to add and subtract two-digit numbers
- Understand that subtraction is the inverse of addition and vice versa; use this to derive and record related addition and subtraction number sentences
- Represent repeated addition and arrays as multiplication, and sharing and repeated subtraction (grouping) as division; use practical and informal written methods and related vocabulary to support multiplication and division, including calculations with remainders
- Use the symbols $+$, $-$, $?$, $\div$ and $=$ to record and interpret number sentences involving all four operations; calculate the value of an unknown in a number sentence (e.g. $\Box \div 2 = 60$, $30 - \Box = 24$).

## Mathematics 5

Understanding shape

- Visualise common 2-D shapes and 3-D solids; identify shapes from pictures of them in different positions and orientations; sort, make and describe shapes, referring to their properties
- Identify reflective symmetry in patterns and 2-D shapes and draw lines of symmetry in shapes
- Follow and give instructions involving position, direction and movement
- Recognise and use whole, half and quarter turns, both clockwise and anticlockwise; know that a right angle represents a quarter turn

## Mathematics 6

Measuring

- Estimate, compare & measure lengths, weights and capacities, choosing & using standard units (m, cm, kg, litre) & suitable measuring instruments
- Read the numbered divisions on a scale, and interpret the divisions between them (e.g. on a scale from 0 to 25 with intervals of 1 shown but only the divisions 0, 5, 10, 15 and 20 numbered); use a ruler to draw and measure lines to the nearest centimetre
- Use units of time (seconds, minutes, hours, days) and know the relationships between them; read the time to the quarter hour; identify time intervals, including those that cross the hour

## Mathematics 7

Handling data

- Answer a question by collecting and recording data in lists and tables; represent the data as block graphs or pictograms to show results; use ICT to organise and present data
- Use lists, tables and diagrams to sort objects; explain choices using appropriate language, including 'not'

# KS1 Programme of Study for Key Stage 1: Science

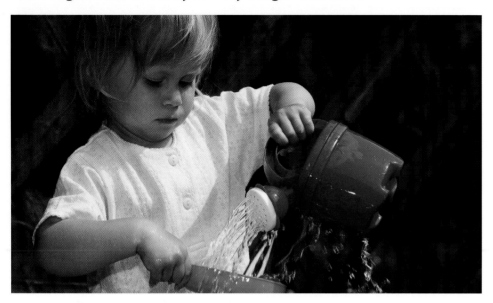

## SC1 Scientific enquiry

| Sc 1.1 | 1.1a | 1.1b | 1.1c | 1.1d |
|---|---|---|---|---|
| Planning | Ask questions 'How?', 'Why?', 'What if?' and decide how they might find answers to them | Use first-hand experience and simple information sources to answer questions | Think about what might happen before deciding what to do | Recognise when a test or comparison is unfair |
| **Sc 1.2** | **1.2a** | **1.2b** | **1.2c** | **1.2d** |
| Ideas and evidence, collecting evidence | Follow simple instructions to control the risks to themselves and to others | Explore using the senses of sight, hearing, smell, touch and taste as appropriate. Make and record observations and measurements | Communicate what happened in a variety of ways including using ICT | |
| **Sc 1.3** | **1.3a** | **1.3b** | **1.3c** | **1.3d** |
| Comparing evidence | Make simple comparisons (eg, hand span, shoe size) and identify simple patterns or associations, and try to explain it, drawing on their knowledge and understanding | Compare what happened with what they expected would happen and try to explain it. Draw on their knowledge and understanding | Review their work and explain what they did to others | |

## SC2 Life processes and living things

| Sc 2.1 | 2.1a | 2.1b | 2.1c | 2.1d |
|---|---|---|---|---|
| Life processes | Differences between things that are living and things that have never been alive | That animals, including humans, move, feed, grow, use their senses and reproduce | Relate life processes to animals and plants found in the local environment | |
| **Sc 2.2** | **2.2a** | **2.2b** | **2.2c** | **2.2d** |
| Ideas and evidence, collecting evidence | Recognise and compare the main external parts of the bodies of humans and other animals | That humans and other animals need food and water to stay alive | That taking exercise and eating the right types and amounts of food help humans to keep healthy | About the role of drugs as medicines |
| | **2.2e** | **2.2f** | **2.2g** | |
| | How to treat animals with care and sensitivity | That humans and other animals can produce off-spring and these off-spring grow into adults | About the senses that enable humans and other animals to be aware of the world around them | |
| **Sc 2.3** | **2.3a** | **2.3b** | **2.3c** | **2.3d** |
| Green plants | Recognise that plants need light and water to grow | To recognise and name the leaf, flowers, stem and root of flowering plants | That seeds grow into flowering plants | |
| **Sc 2.4** | **2.4a** | **2.4b** | | |
| Variation and classification | Recognise similarities and differences between themselves and others, and to treat others with sensitivity | Group living things according to observable similarities and differences | | |
| **Sc 2.5** | **2.5a** | **2.5b** | **2.5c** | |
| Living things in their environment | Find out about the different kinds of plants and animals in the local environment | Identify similarities & differences between local environments & ways in which these affect animals & plants that are found there | Care for the environment | |

## SC3 Materials and their properties

| Sc 3.1<br>Grouping materials | 3.1a | 3.1b | 3.1c | 3.1d |
|---|---|---|---|---|
| | Use their senses to explore and recognise the similarities and differences between materials | Sort objects into groups on the basis of their properties: texture, float, hardness and transparency and whether they are magnetic or non-magnetic | Recognise and name common types of material and recognise that some of them are found naturally | Find out about the uses of a variety of materials and how these are chosen for specific uses on the basis of their simple properties |

| Sc 3.2<br>Changing materials | 3.2a | 3.2b | | |
|---|---|---|---|---|
| | Find out how the shapes of objects made from some materials can be changed by some processes including squashing, bending, twisting and stretching | Explore and describe the way some everyday materials, e.g. water, chocolate, bread and clay, change when they are heated or cooled | | |

## SC4 Physical processes

| Sc 4.1<br>Electricity | 4.1a | 4.1b | 4.1c | 4.1d |
|---|---|---|---|---|
| | About everyday appliances that use electricity | Simple series circuits involving batteries, wires, bulbs and other components e.g. buzzers | How a switch can be used to break a circuit | Recognise when a test or comparison is unfair |

| Sc 4.2<br>Forces and motion | 4.2a | 4.2b | 4.2c | |
|---|---|---|---|---|
| | Find out about and describe the movement of familiar things e.g. cars going faster, slowing down, changing direction | That both pushes and pulls are examples of forces | To recognise that when things speed up, slow down, or change direction there is a cause | |

| Sc 4.3<br>Light and sound | 4.3a | 4.3b | 4.3c | 4.3d |
|---|---|---|---|---|
| | Identify different light sources including the sun | That darkness is the absence of light | That there are many kinds of sound and sources of sound | That sounds travel away from sources, getting fainter as they do so, and that they are heard |

# KS1 Programmes of Study

## History

| H 1 | 1a | 1b | 1c |
|---|---|---|---|
| Chronological understanding | Place events and objects in chronological order | Use common words and phrases relating to the passing of time e.g. before, after, a long time ago and past | Retrieve information that has been stored |
| **H 2** | **2a** | **2b** | |
| Knowledge & understanding of events people and changes | Recognise why people did things, why events happened and what happened as a result | Identify differences between ways of life at different times | |
| **H 3** | **3a** | | |
| Historical interpretation | Identify different ways in which the past is represented | | |
| **H 4** | **4a** | **4b** | |
| Historical enquiry | Find out about the past from a range of sources of information | Ask and answer questions about the past | |
| **H 5** | **5a** | | |
| Organisation and communication | Select from their knowledge of history and communicate it in a variety of ways | | |
| **H 6** | **6a** | **6b** | **6c** | **6d** |
| Breadth of study | Changes in their own lives and the way of life of their family or others around them | The way of life of people in the more distant past who lived in the local area or elsewhere in Britain | The lives of significant men, women or children | Past events from the history of Britain and the wider world |

## Design and Technology

| D&T 1 | 1a | 1b | 1c | 1d | 1e |
|---|---|---|---|---|---|
| Developing, planning and communicating ideas | Generate ideas by drawing on their own and other people's experiences | Develop ideas by hoping materials and putting together components | Talk about their ideas | Plan by suggesting what to do next as their ideas develop | Communicate ideas using a variety of materials including drawing and making moulds |
| **D&T 2** | **2a** | **2b** | **2c** | **2d** | **2e** |
| Working with tools, equipment and materials | Explore sensory qualities of materials | Measure, mark out, cut and shape | Assemble, join and combine materials | Use simple finishing techniques | Follow safe procedures |
| **D&T 3** | **3a** | **3b** | | | |
| Evaluating processes and products | Talk about their ideas | Identify improvements | | | |
| **D&T 4** | **4a** | **4b** | | | |
| Knowledge & understanding of materials and components | Working characteristics of materials | How mechanisms can be used | | | |
| **D&T 5** | **5a** | **5b** | **5c** | | |
| Breadth of study | Focused practical tasks | Design and make assignments | Investigate and evaluate products | | |

## Geography

| G 1.1 | 1.1a | 1.1b | 1.1c | 1.1d | |
|---|---|---|---|---|---|
| Geographical enquiry | Ask geographical questions | Observe and record | Express their own views about people, places, and environments | Communicate in different ways | |
| G 1.2 | 1.2a | 1.2b | 1.2c | 1.2d | |
| Geographical skills | Use geographical vocabulary | Use fieldwork skills | Use globes, maps and plans at a range of scales | Use secondary sources of information | |
| G 2 | 2a | 2b | 2c | 2d | 2e |
| Knowledge and understanding of places | Identify and describe what places are like | Identify and describe what places are | Recognise how places become they way they are & how they are changing | Recognise how places compare with other places | Recognise how places are linked to other places in the world |
| G 3 | 3a | 3b | 3c | 3d | |
| Knowledge & understanding of patterns & processes | Make observations about where things are located | Recognise changes in physical & human features | | | |
| G 4 | 4a | 4b | | | |
| Knowledge & understanding of environment | Recognise changes in the environment | Recognise how the environment may be improved & sustained | | | |
| G 5 | 5a | 5b | 5c | 5d | |
| Breadth of study | The locality of the school | A contrasting locality in the UK or overseas | Study at a local scale | Carry out fieldwork investigations outside the classroom | |

## ICT

| ICT 1.1 | 1.1a | 1.1b | 1.1c | 1.1d |
|---|---|---|---|---|
| Finding things out | Gather information from a variety of sources | Enter and store information in a variety of forms | Retrieve information that has been stored | |
| ICT 1.2 | 1.2a | 1.2b | 1.2c | 1.2d |
| Developing ideas and making things happen | Use text, tables, images and sound to develop their ideas | Select from and add to information thay have rerieved for particular purposes | Plan and give instructions to make things happen | Try things out and explore what happens in real and imaginary instructions |
| ICT 2 | 2a | 2b | | |
| Exchanging and sharing information | Share their ideas by presenting information in a variety of forms | Present their completed work effectively | | |

## Physical Education

| PE 1 | 1a | 1b | |
|---|---|---|---|
| Aquiring and developing skills | Explore basic skills, actions and ideas with increasing understanding | Remember and repeat simple skills & actions with increasing control | |
| PE 2 | 2a | 2b | 2c |
| Selecting and applying skills, tactics and compositional ideas | Explore how to choose and apply skills and actions in sequence & in combination | Vary the way they perform skills by using simple tactics and movement phrases | Apply rules and conventions for different activities |
| PE 3 | 3a | 3b | 3c |
| Evaluating and improving performance | Describe what they have done | Observe, describe & copy what others have done | Use what they have learnt to improve the quality and control of their work |
| PE 4 | 4a | 4b | |
| Knowledge and understanding of fitness and health | How important it is to be active | Recognise and describe how their bodies feel during different activities | |
| PE 5 | 5a | 5b | 5c |
| Breadth of study | Dance | Games | Gymnastics |

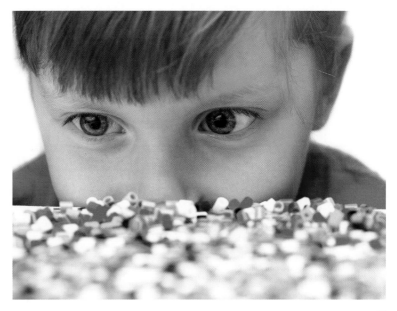

## Art and Design

| A&D 1 | 1a | 1b | | |
|---|---|---|---|---|
| Exploring and developing ideas | Record from first hand observation, experience & imagination | Ask and answer questions about the starting points for their work | | |
| **A&D 2** | **2a** | **2b** | **2c** | |
| Investigating and making art, craft and design | Investigate the possibilities of materials and processes | Try out tools and techniques and apply these | Represent observations, ideas and feelings | |
| **A&D 3** | **3a** | **3b** | | |
| Evaluating and developing work | Review what they and others have done | Identify what they might change | | |
| **A&D 4** | **4a** | **4b** | **4c** | |
| Knowledge and understanding of materials and components | Visual and tactile elements | Materials and processes used in making art, craft and design | Differences and similarities in the work of artists, craftspeople and designers | |
| **A&D 5** | **5a** | **5b** | **5c** | **5d** |
| Breadth of study | Exploring a range of starting points | Working on their own and collaborating with others | Using a range of materials and processes | Investigating different types of art, craft and design |

## Music

| M 1 | 1a | 1b | 1c | |
|---|---|---|---|---|
| Performing skills | Use their voices expressively by singing songs, chants, rhymes | Play tuned and untuned instruments | Rehearse and perform with others | |
| **M 2** | **2a** | **2b** | | |
| Composing skills | Create musical patterns | Explore, choose and organise sounds and musical ideas | | |
| **M 3** | **3a** | **3b** | | |
| Responding and reviewing — appraising skills | Explore and express their ideas and feelings about music | Make improvements to their own work | | |
| **M 4** | **4a** | **4b** | **4c** | |
| Responding and reviewing — listening skills | Listen with concentration and internalise & recall sounds | How combined musical elements can be organised | How sounds can be made in different ways | |
| **M 5** | **5a** | **5b** | **5c** | **5d** |
| Breadth of study | A range of musical activities | Responding to a range of starting points | Working on their own, in groups and as a class | A range of live and recorded music |

**PSHE: non-statutory guidance**

| PSHE 1 | 1a | 1b | 1c | 1d | 1e | | | |
|---|---|---|---|---|---|---|---|---|
| Developing confidence & responsibility & making the most of their abilities | Recognise their likes and dislikes, what is fair and unfair, what is right and wrong | Share their opinions on things that matter to them and their views | Recognise, name and deal with their feelings in a positive way | Think about themselves, learn from their experiences and recognise what they are good at | How to set simple goals | | | |
| **PSHE 2** | **2a** | **2b** | **2c** | **2d** | **2e** | **2f** | **2g** | |
| Preparing to play an active role as citizens | Take part in discussions with one other person and the whole class | Take part in a simple debate about topical issues | Recognise choices they make, and the difference between right and wrong | Realise that people and other living things have needs, and that they have responsibilities to meet them | That they belong to various groups and communities, such as a family | What improves and harms their local, natural & built environments | Contribute to the life of the class and school | Realise that money comes from different sources |
| **PSHE 3** | **3a** | **3b** | **3c** | **3d** | **3e** | **3f** | **3g** | |
| Developing a healthier lifestyle | Make simple choices that improve their health and wellbeing | Maintain personal hygiene | How some diseases spread and can be controlled | About the process of growing from young to old and how people's needs change | Name the main parts of the body | That household products and medicines can be harmful | Rules for, and ways of, keeping safe, basic road safety | |
| **PSHE 4** | **4a** | **4b** | **4c** | **4d** | **4e** | | | |
| Developing good relationships and respecting differences | Recognise how their behaviour affects other people | Listen to other people and play and work co-operatively | Identify and respect differences and similarities between people | That family and friends should care for each other | That there are different types of teasing and bullying, that bullying is wrong | | | |